AARP
Tablets
tech to connect

by Corey Sandler

WILEY

John Wiley & Sons, Inc.

AARP Tablets: Tech to Connect

Published by
John Wiley & Sons, Inc.
111 River Street
Hoboken, NJ 07030-5774

www.wiley.com

WILEY

Tech to Connect: Tablets

Unlike your kids and grandkids, you probably didn't grow up glued to high-tech gadgets. You might even still be using that bulky computer on your desk. Now there's another option: tablets. Those light, portable computers give you the freedom to plug in wherever you are.

If you're feeling overwhelmed by your choices, or intimidated by the new technology, this book is for you.

Dedicated to helping you live your best life — stay connected with your friends, family, and community; and stretch your money — AARP has joined with Dummies to offer this how-to guide.

This easy-to-understand resource offers an introduction to using tablets physically (how and what to tap, swipe, and pinch) and otherwise (as a Web browser, a phone, or a video camera); step-by-step instructions for doing everything from downloading apps and free eBooks to connecting with WiFi networks; and ways to protect your security whether you're at home or on the road.

So come on board. Let us be your guide.

AARP is a nonprofit, nonpartisan membership organization that helps people 50 and older improve their lives. For more than 50 years, AARP has been serving our members and society by creating positive social change. AARP's mission is to enhance the quality of life for all as we age; lead positive social change; and deliver value to members through information, service and advocacy.

About the Author

Corey Sandler is a voracious reader and an indefatigable author of books. Also magazines and, ages ago, newspapers. He has written more than 170 books: computers and technology as well as history, sports, and business. Sandler travels all over the world as a public speaker, lecturing aboard some of the world's most luxurious cruise lines in some of the world's most glamorous or most obscure places.

He studied journalism (and took some courses to program a gigantic mainframe computer) at Syracuse University. He began his career as a daily newspaper reporter in Ohio and then New York, moving on to a post as a correspondent for The Associated Press. From there he joined Ziff-Davis Publishing as the first executive editor of *PC Magazine*. He wrote his first book about computers in 1983 and hasn't come close to stopping.

When he's not on the road and living on his smartphone and computer, he's at home on Nantucket island 30 miles out to sea off the coast of Massachusetts. He shares his life with his wife Janice; their two grown children have their own careers elsewhere on the continent.

You can see Sandler's current list of books on his website at sandlerbooks. com. You can send an email to him at TechToConnect@sandlerbooks. com or through the links you find on the website. He promises to respond to courteous inquiries as quickly as he can. Spam, on the other hand, will go back into the can where it belongs.

Dedication

To my wife and family, always there to connect me when most needed.

Author's Acknowledgments

A book may have one name on the cover, but it is always the product of a team. And I have once again benefited from the professional assistance of some of the best.

Thanks to Katie Mohr and the publishing team at Wiley, and to editor *par excellence* Tonya Maddox Cupp. And thanks to you for buying and reading this book: Though the subject may be high tech, the connection between us is old school.

Publisher's Acknowledgments

We're proud of this book; please send us your comments at http://dummies.custhelp.com. For other comments, please contact our Customer Care Department within the U.S. at 877-762-2974, outside the U.S. at 317-572-3993, or fax 317-572-4002.

Some of the people who helped bring this book to market include the following:

Acquisitions and Editorial

Editor: Tonya Maddox Cupp

Senior Acquisitions Editor: Katie Mohr

Editorial Manager: Jodi Jensen

Editorial Assistant: Amanda Graham

Sr. Editorial Assistant: Cherie Case

Cover Photo: ©Darren Kemper / Corbis

Composition Services

Project Coordinator: Kristie Rees

Layout and Graphics: Jennifer Mayberry

Proofreaders: Debbye Butler, Melissa Cossell, Susan Moritz

Indexer: BIM Indexing & Proofreading Services

Publishing and Editorial for Technology Dummies

Richard Swadley, Vice President and Executive Group Publisher

Andy Cummings, Vice President and Publisher

Mary Bednarek, Executive Acquisitions Director

Mary C. Corder, Editorial Director

Publishing for Consumer Dummies

Kathleen Nebenhaus, Vice President and Executive Publisher

Composition Services

Debbie Stailey, Director of Composition Services

Contents at a Glance

Table of Contents

Introduction

When I was born, radio was king. Big hulking wooden boxes produced static-filled sound from live orchestras and the occasional breaking news event. My grandmother had a set that included a shortwave receiver; on a clear night we could pick up snatches of news from Europe and the mysterious clicks and beeps of Morse code: They had to be spies.

Our family had one of the first black-and-white television sets in our circle of friends: Rabbit ears pulled in three or four channels of basic entertainment. Uncle Miltie, Rod Serling, and Playhouse 90 were among my touchstones. We had a phone. It was hard-wired into a wall outlet in the kitchen. Owned by Ma Bell, it came with a rotary dial; to make a long-distance call, we dialed the operator and made arrangements, but only after careful consideration of the cost.

When we traveled, we made sure to carry a few dimes so that we could make a call from a phone booth, one of which was on nearly every corner in a big city or inside most candy stores, restaurants, and stores. And computers? Owned by the government and huge corporations, they were the size of houses. Fronted by panels of dials, switches, and blinking lights, they were tended to by technicians in white lab coats, feeding them stacks of punch cards.

When I went off to college, my heroes included newspaper writers like Harrison Salisbury and James Reston. And there were Edward R. Murrow and Walter Cronkite, who helped define radio and then television journalism. And I also loved toys. We didn't much use the word *technology* back then, but I was fascinated by anything that had a power cord or a battery. I was one of the only journalism students who also spent time in the basement of the engineering building on campus, home to one of those huge, whirring, clicking IBM mainframe computers.

I went on to a career as a reporter for daily newspapers and then a correspondent for The Associated Press. In 1981, the world changed with the introduction of the first IBM PC; I was present at its birth and became the first executive editor of the pioneering publication *PC Magazine*.

About This Book

Now here's the truly amazing thing: The hottest new piece of high technology is a small device that squeezes a bunch of gee-whiz features into a little piece of plastic and glass that weighs about a pound.

It's called a tablet.

Many people who are new to this particular corner of the technological world may look around and see an Amazon Kindle in one corner of the living room and an Apple iPad in the other and think they are the same thing. An original Kindle (and its similar cousins, a NOOK, Sony Reader, and Kobo) is basically a device that does one thing: It reads eBooks.

A tablet can read eBooks. But it can also do this:

- Connect to the Internet and display all the web pages you're used to visiting. You can buy things, do your banking, and browse to your heart's content.
- Send and receive email just as you can on a large computer or a tiny smart-phone.
- Listen to music that is stored in digital form.
- Watch videos downloaded to your tablet or "streamed" over the Internet.
- Shoot, store, or send still photos or videos.
- Set up a video or audio conference to connect to friends, family, and associates anywhere in the world. With your tablet you can also make a phone call.
- Play games, from fast-action adventures to more cerebral pursuits like chess, sudoku, and crossword puzzles.
- Communicate with overhead satellites or nearby cell towers to tell you where you are and give you turn-by-turn directions to a specific address.

Who This Book Is For

I'm involved in what they call high technology. I've been amongst the first users and explainers of nearly every new type of television, telephone, and computer ever since.

Now allow me to describe my children. They are both grown, off on their own adventures in life, and more or less independent. They were born in an age where color television, simple personal computers, and basic cellphones were everywhere and anywhere. They do not know a world without the Internet. Their music, entertainment, and all the personal details of their lives exist within the platters of a computer. Neither one of them has ever used a dial to place a phone call. They easily navigate the world of PCs, Macs, iPods, iPads, BlackBerry and Android smartphones and tablets, digital cameras, and GPS mapping devices.

In thinking about this book, I made the assumption that you, dear reader, are probably somewhere in the middle between my experience and my children's.

Like me, you were there as these modern devices invaded. But perhaps unlike me, you were more on the sidelines as our world changed. You've almost certainly used a computer on some level or another: at work or in a library or at an ATM. You may even be a whiz on the Internet and a champ at email. You've owned many cameras (film, though, is so last century) and probably a video camera or two. And the basics of a GPS are somewhat familiar to you.

Dozens of brands are on the market. There isn't space to cover steps for every possible brand, so I focus on three of the most popular. These instructions generally often apply to other brands. As I wrote this book, I concentrated on three typical devices:

- Apple iPad
- BlackBerry PlayBook
- Samsung Galaxy Tab

I concentrate on the similarities and point out the relatively few important differences amongst them.

Conventions Used in This Book

These details will help you use the book:

- Sometimes you will see icons in the margin. Icons are just small versions of menu or program graphics. The thing you see to the left? That's an icon. Some icons are pointed out in pictures, too.

- Terminology: The pictures throughout the book are referred to as figures. A web page is the same thing as a website. The Internet is the same thing as the web.

- Sometimes you'll see a graphic like the one shown to the left of this bullet. This graphic is a way to draw your attention to information that I think is particularly useful to have. Maybe it's a way to save time, or your own hide.

How This Book Is Organized

This book has 13 chapters. You can dip in and out of this reference as you see fit; you are not required to read it from cover to cover. If there's a topic you're interested in right now, check the table of contents in the front of the book, or the index at the back. If there's nothing pressing right now, skim through and see what interests you at this point. You probably know how you'd like to use your tablet. This book can tell you how to start that. Once you get a handle on whatever that is (setting up email, recording and sending videos, or buying and downloading eBooks, for instance), poke around and see what untapped talents your tablet has.

Chapter 1

Using the Touchscreen

We came of age in the day of the manual typewriter. Remember the process? Roll in a piece of paper, hit the return bar a few times, and then pound the daylights out of the keys. On a tablet, everything is virtual. When you need a keyboard, one will appear on the screen and you can tap its pretend keys. You use your fingers directly on the screen.

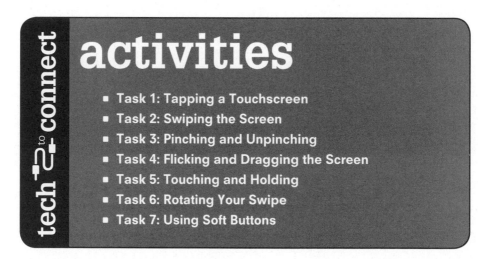

tech to connect

activities

- Task 1: Tapping a Touchscreen
- Task 2: Swiping the Screen
- Task 3: Pinching and Unpinching
- Task 4: Flicking and Dragging the Screen
- Task 5: Touching and Holding
- Task 6: Rotating Your Swipe
- Task 7: Using Soft Buttons

Task 1: Tapping a Touchscreen

One of the basic touchscreen commands is a simple tap. Think of a tap as similar to a mouse click on a computer.

When you tap, you can do one of these tasks depending on the situation:

- Select an object. In certain situations, a tap highlights a virtual onscreen button or lets you indicate choices. See Figure 1-1.

- Call up the virtual onscreen keyboard. Tap in a text box to reveal the keys so you can enter addresses or the like.

- Open an application. Tap a shortcut on the home screen to start that program or go online to the connected web link.

- Choose an item from a list. For example, in a music or video player you'll see small pictures (thumbnails) or a list of items; tap one to make it start playing.

- Select an article or a product from a web page. For example, when you're reading the front page of an online newspaper, you can tap a headline or a photo to open the full article for reading.

- Tell the web browser to go to a page. Tap a link to visit a web page.

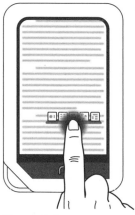

Figure 1-1

Knock, knock: Double-tapping

A double-tap, two fast touches to the screen, is different from a single tap. When you double-tap, you might zoom in to (enlarge) a photo on a website. Double-tapping again usually makes the image the original size. Do the same with a map or text. Depending on what you're enlarging or reducing, it may take a second for the page to resolve or come into focus. The amount of enlargement or reduction is preset by the system; for more precise control, use pinch or unpinch (spread) gestures.

Task 2: Swiping the Screen

Swiping means touching one finger to the screen and keeping it in contact with the screen as you move. See Figure 1-2.

Here is what you can do when you swipe, depending on the situation:

- Unlock or wake up a sleeping tablet. (A tablet can be set up to automatically turn off or "sleep" after a few minutes of inactivity to save battery power.) Apple iPad and BlackBerry PlayBook: Swipe across or up the screen to wake up a sleeping tablet. Android devices: Touch the unlock button and swipe across the screen to make the device useable.

- Drag an object from one point to another. On all tablets, you can rearrange many objects on the home screen and within certain applications. Chapter 13 explains how to do the former.

- Scroll through a list. Touch the down arrow or touch one of the items in a list and keep your finger on the screen as you move it down (to start) or up.

- Switch between views of installed apps and utilities on a BlackBerry PlayBook. Swipe left or right in the lower part of the home screen. The views change between All, Favorites, Media, Games, or BlackBerry Bridge.

Figure 1-2

Task 3: Pinching and Unpinching

You may think your iPad or your PlayBook or your Tab is almost too cute to bear. But I'm not proposing you pinch it like a baby's cheek. Perform a pinch (and its opposite, an unpinch or a spread) with two fingers. Most people use their thumb and pointing finger. See Figure 1-3.

To reduce the size of an already enlarged image or website, place two fingers on the screen and then move them toward each other. To enlarge an image or website, place two fingers close together on the screen and then move them away from each other.

Figure 1-3

Clean up your act

Sorry to have to break this to you, but your fingers are oily. As you touch the screen, you are likely to leave behind streaks. It's not a big deal: Wipe the screen with a soft cloth like the one you use to clean your eyeglasses.

Task 4: Flicking and Dragging the Screen

Have you ever dispatched an ant from the picnic table with a beautifully exercised flick of your finger? There are no ants on most tablets, but the flick gesture is a valuable one.

Here's what a flick can do, depending on your situation:

- Scroll quickly through long lists. To stop the rapid scroll, tap the screen.
- Zoom through emails, songs, videos, and pictures. See Figure 1-4 of an example of a song list.
- On the BlackBerry PlayBook: Make smaller or close an open web page or application.

‹ Music	🎵 All Songs		Search All 🔍
1			
🎵 10,000 Maniacs Who Knows Where Time...	Unknown	Unknown	4:45
5			
500_Miles Roger McGuinn	Roger McGuinn	Folk Den Podcast	3:39
A			
🎵 Alison Krause I Will	Unknown	Unknown	4:04
🎵 Allison Krause I Don't Believe You've Me...	Unknown	Unknown	3:09
B			
🎵 Bonnie Raitt Any Day Woman	Unknown	Unknown	2:23
E			
Eire Canal	Roger McGuinn	Folkden	3:09
F			
🎵 Farewell, Angelina	Joan Baez	Bowery Songs	3:37
J			
🎵 Joan Baez Baby Blue (Bowery Songs)	Unknown	Unknown	4:29

Figure 1-4

A drag is kind of like the opposite of a flick. You can drag by pressing your finger against a spot on the screen and moving your finger slowly without lifting it.

You may need to touch and hold your finger in place on an object for a second or two before you can move it; the object will glow or change size when it's ready to be swiped. Release your finger and then reapply it to the object and drag it to a new location.

Here's what a drag (what a drag!) can do for you on all tablets:

■ Move a web page or image left or right or up or down. You may need to do that when it's too large to see all of it on the screen.

■ Go from place to place on a map.

Task 5: Touching and Holding (Long Press)

What a nice thought, all cuddly and romantic. Touching and holding, sometimes also referred to as a long press, does different things on different tablets. On most tablets, touching and holding your finger on an object for a second or so changes the item so you can move it. See Figure 1-5.

On some tablets, a small screen will show a Delete button. On Android devices, touching and holding your finger on a blank part of the home screen will display a new menu that lets you customize that display. On the BlackBerry PlayBook, a gesture can reveal menu options or open web links in a new tab.

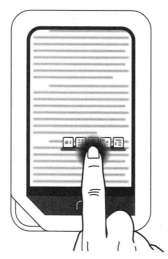

Figure 1-5

Task 6: Rotating Your Swipe

I am referring to this gesture as a rotating swipe. It turns a picture to a new angle, anywhere from a slight adjustment one direction or the other to a 90, 180, or 270-degree flip. Here's how:

1. On an iPad or Android device, plant your thumb in one place on an image.
2. With your thumb still down, touch your pointer finger (some call it the index finger) elsewhere on the screen.
3. Keep your thumb where it is, but move your finger clockwise or counter-clockwise around it. The image will follow along as you rotate.

Swiping from the Frame

The BlackBerry PlayBook has an active frame, or bezel, surrounding the touchscreen. Different gestures that involve the frame will show the home screen, reveal a menu, switch between or close applications, or bring up the status bar.

Task 7: Using Soft Buttons

Some tablets, including the Samsung Galaxy Tab, have actual buttons. They are physically there, but they can change function in certain circumstances. Just to make things interesting, soft buttons are sometimes called command keys. The basic set of four icons are explained in Table 1-1. You can see them on the tablet in Figure 1-6.

Menu | Back

Home | Search

Figure 1-6

Table 1-1		The Basics Icons
Icon	*Name*	*Instructions*
▤	Menu	Press once to display options that depend on what you're doing right then. Press again to dismiss the menu.
⌂	Home	Press once to go back to the home screen. Or, press and hold to list recent applications.
↰	Back	Press once to go back a screen, close the current application, or dismiss the keyboard.
◯	Search	Press once to open the tablet or web search page. Or, press and hold to open Voice Search.

Chapter 2

Typing on the Virtual Keyboard

When is a keyboard not a keyboard? When it has no keys. Most current tablets have a virtual onscreen keyboard. When you need to enter text or numbers, the keyboard magically appears. When you don't need it, it's not there. And because the keyboard is virtual — made up entirely of dots of light illuminated on the screen — it can change.

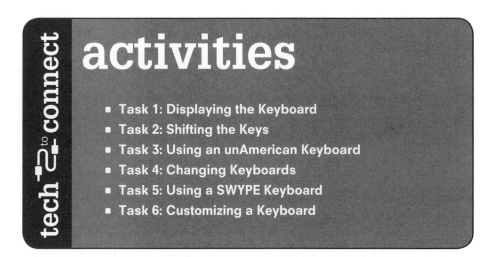

activities

tech to connect

- Task 1: Displaying the Keyboard
- Task 2: Shifting the Keys
- Task 3: Using an unAmerican Keyboard
- Task 4: Changing Keyboards
- Task 5: Using a SWYPE Keyboard
- Task 6: Customizing a Keyboard

Task 1: Displaying the Keyboard

Displaying the keyboard is simple. Do this anytime you're on a screen where you have to fill in letters or numbers:

1. Tap in a box like the one you see in Figure 2-1. The basic keyboard will appear and look much like what you see in Figure 2-2.
2. Type away. If you need a special character or number, tap one of the shift keys.
3. When you are finished, tap the Go or Return key. Or, on certain tablets, tap the close keyboard button (which is pointed out in Figure 2-2).

When the keyboard first appears, it usually shows lowercase letters. Sometimes things are set up so that the first character you type is automatically capitalized (even if you are typing on the lowercase keyboard). On most keyboards, if you press and hold a character for a second, a small menu of secondary characters and symbols comes up. To switch to the uppercase keyboard, tap the upward arrow or aA button; for symbols, tap the SYM or 123 button.

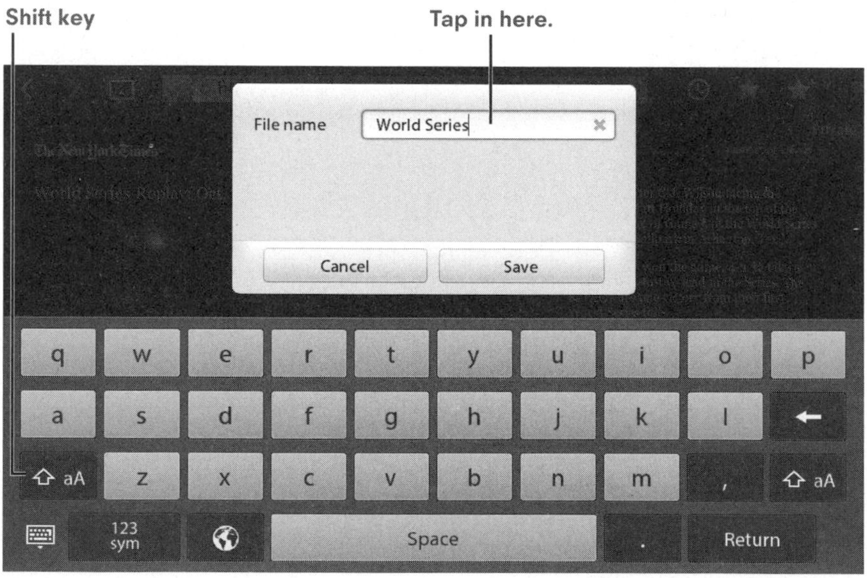

Shift key   Tap in here.

Figure 2-1

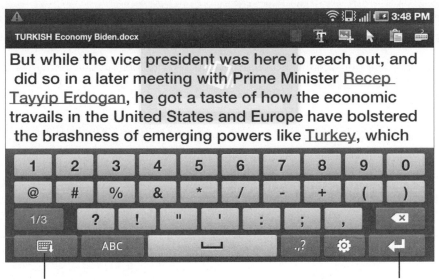

Close keyboard button   Return key

Figure 2-2

Task 2: Shifting the Keys

Tapping the shift or up arrow gives you capital letters or special symbols. See Figure 2-3.

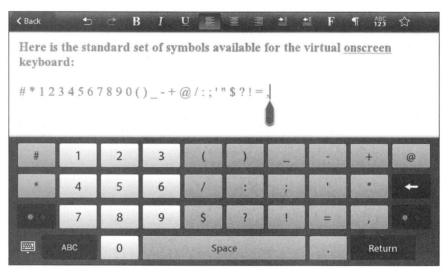

Figure 2-3

Inside voices

I knew a woman who was incapable of dealing with the concept of the shift key on a typewriter. Whenever she sent a message, it would either be all lowercase letters, which was a bit confusing, or it was ALL CAPITAL LETTERS ALL THE TIME, WHICH MADE IT FEEL AS IF SHE WAS ALWAYS SHOUTING AT ME. It hurt my ears to read her notes; don't type in all caps.

Here's how to shift from one type of character to another:

1. To make the next character a capital letter, tap the shift key (which usually has an up arrow). Figure 2-4 points out the shift key.

2. To type only capital letters (until you decide you want to do otherwise), do one of the following steps:

   ■ **Apple iPad.** Double-tap the shift (up arrow) key. It will turn blue; it will keep giving you capital letters until you tap it (once) again.

   ■ **BlackBerry PlayBook.** Press and hold the aA shift key for a second. The button will be surrounded by blue. All characters will be capitals until you tap the shift key again to return to its standard setting.

   ■ **Android devices.** Press and hold the upward arrow shift key for a second. The button will turn solid blue. All characters will be capitals until you tap the key again.

3. To enter just about any $#%&! symbol, as well as less common ones like €£¥¿¡, tap the shift key or use submenus.

   ■ **Apple iPad.** Tap the symbol shift key labeled #+= or 123 or .?123. The specific symbol key may differ between applications, and there may be secondary groups of symbols available from secondary keyboards. Tap the ABC key to return to the standard keyboard.

   ■ **BlackBerry PlayBook.** Tap the 123sym button to see the first set of characters. Tap the blue dot key to see the second set. Tap the ABC key to return to the standard keyboard. In some cases, the standard keyboard hides special characters. For example, press and hold the lowercase o to open a submenu with these choices: ò ó ô õ ö ø. Tap the one you want to insert. See Figure 2-4.

   ■ **Samsung Galaxy Tab.** Tap the SYM key to display a basic keyboard. Some letters offer special characters. For example, the S character also shows a small $; tap and hold the S in lowercase or uppercase to display a submenu with these additional choices: S Š ™ β $ §. Tap the 123 button to display more numbers and symbols. Move from one to the next by tapping again in that same box, or return to standard characters with a tap of the ABC button.

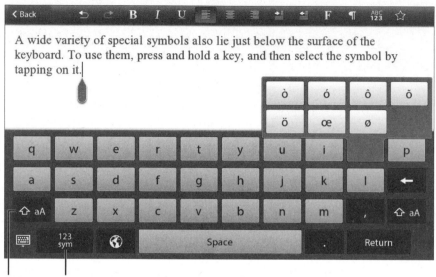

Figure 2-4

Shift key   Number and symbol shift key

On the Apple iPad, you need to lock caps before the keyboard will respond to a double-tap on the shift key. Tap the settings icon (which is usually a gear on the first home screen), and tap General, and then tap Keyboard. Tap the Enable Caps Lock item. If you want to disable this function, go back to the Settings panel and turn off caps lock.

Task 3: Using an unAmerican Keyboard

If you speak a language other than American English, or if you need to send a message to someone who does, on most tablets you can select from a range of virtual onscreen keyboards that include accents, diacritical marks, and additional characters.

Here's how to select a foreign language keyboard for your Apple iPad:

1. Tap Settings and then tap General.
2. Tap Keyboard and then tap International Keyboards.
3. Tap Add New Keyboard.
4. Flick through the list to select the keyboard you want to use. You can enable as many international keyboards as you want, but you can use only one of them at a time.

To change keyboard languages while you're using an Apple iPad application, do this step:

1. Tap the small international keyboard button between the toggle and space-bar.
2. Keep tapping as many times as necessary to get to the one you want. Eventually you come full circle to the one you started from.

If you're using a BlackBerry PlayBook, you can change from one keyboard to another anytime the virtual onscreen keyboard is in use.

1. Tap the international keyboard button (shown in Figure 2-5) to display a menu.
2. Tap within the menu.
3. Swipe up or down until you come to the keyboard you want to use. Then tap its name.

Tap to change keyboard.
(International keyboard)

Figure 2-5

If you have a Samsung Galaxy Tab, switching from one keyboard to another is quite easy:

1. Anytime a keyboard is on the screen, look for a shift icon above one of the characters that indicates the current language. For example, EN is above the letter Q on the U.S. English keyboard; FR is above the letter A on the French keyboard.

2. Make a long press on the character and then choose the language you want to use.

Task 4: Changing Keyboards

What in the world is a QWERTY? Nothing, really. The word comes from the first six letters of the standard U.S. English keyboard. Sometimes, when you change from one language character set to another, the tablet automatically reconfigures the keyboard.

If not, here's how to specify a non-QWERTY keyboard:

1. Tap the settings or setup icon. It is usually on the home screen and the icon is usually a gear. See Figure 2-6.
2. Tap Input or Keyboard.
3. Tap one of the choices.

Settings icon

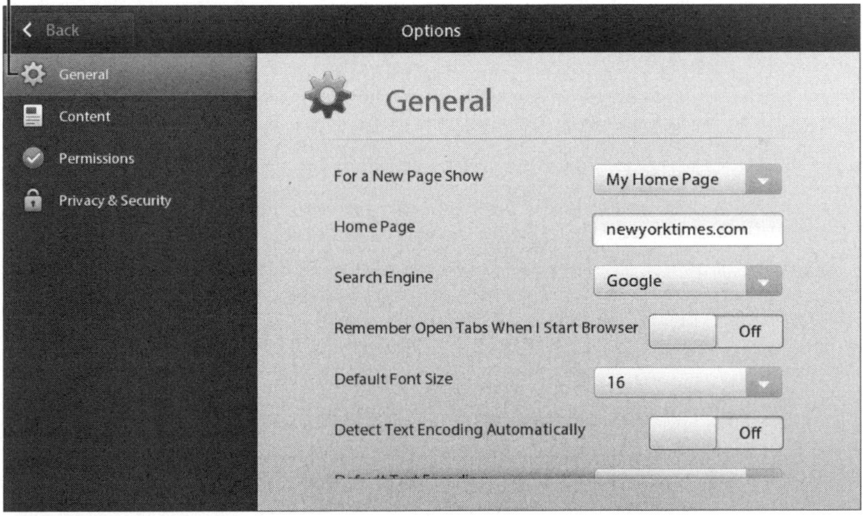

Figure 2-6

Task 5: Using a Swype Keyboard

The Swype and a few other, similar, concepts have been around for a while in various forms, but only now is it reaching the point where you may find it quicker than tapping individual letters. The Swype system is now on Samsung Galaxy devices and is expected to be on other tablets in coming years. Most systems will slightly alter the virtual onscreen keyboard to include a swoopy S alongside the SYM shift key to tell you that Swype is available. See Figure 2-7.

You may find it easier to use the Swype system if you hold your tablet in landscape mode, which gives you a larger keyboard to work with. Tap and hold the swoopy S to go to tips on how to better use Swype.

Here's how to use a Swype keyboard:

1. Go to the settings menu for the keyboard or go to the main settings control panel. On most tablets, tapping places a check mark and turns on Swype. See Figure 2-8.

2. To write a word, touch its first letter and keep in contact with the screen as you start moving in the direction of the next character.

3. When you reach the next character, pause for a second, change course, and head for the next character. Make an extra small loop within a character if you want to double that letter.

4. When you are done typing, just lift your finger. The system shows the word it thinks you just drew. If it is uncertain, you will see several options; just tap the correct one.

To begin a word with a capital, do one of these three:

■ Tap the upward arrow shift key before you start spelling. Only the first character will be capitalized.

■ Press and hold the upward arrow shift button for a moment before you start spelling. The keyboard locks into all capital letters until the next time you tap the shift button.

■ Slide your trace path above the top row of the keyboard and then continue to the next letters. Any letter that you type after your finger has gone above the top row is capitalized.

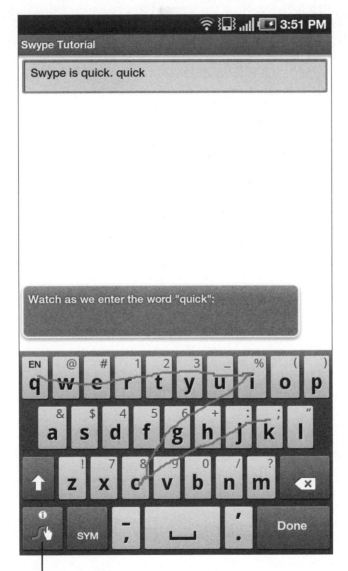

Swype is available

Figure 2-7

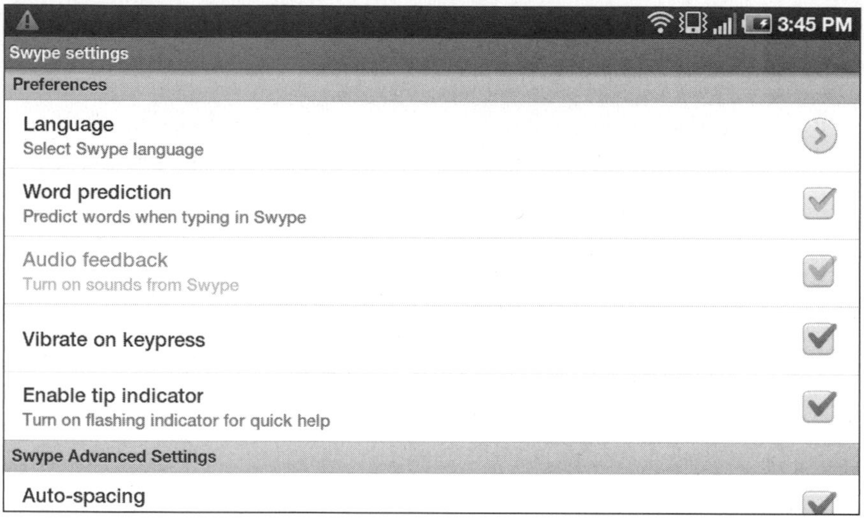

Figure 2-8

To quickly change between the standard tapping keyboard and the Swype keyboard, just press and hold anywhere on the screen where it expects you to type in characters: in a memo, word processing, email or text message, or web browser address line. Tap Input Method, and then tap either Swype or Keyboard.

Take a Swype at it

Swype technology actually works, although it's up to you to decide whether it represents an actual improvement over tapping. In my opinion, it does speed up my text entry (and web searches), but it comes at the cost of an enhanced level of focus; in other words, I have to devote a bit more attention to what I am doing when I choose to Swype instead of type.

Task 6: Customizing a Keyboard

Your tablet's virtual keyboard can morph itself into something other than the usual QWERTY board. (A QWERTY is named for the first six letters of its alphabet row. There are versions in use in Europe and Asia that are slightly different. See Figure 2-9.) You also can customize your keyboard.

Here's how to customize your keyboard:

1. Tap the settings app. Or, tap the Settings menu. On the BlackBerry PlayBook, swipe down from the tablet's top frame.
2. Tap the keyboard you want to use.
3. On some tablets, including the Android-based Samsung Galaxy Tab, you can turn on or off features like these:

   ■ Automatic full stop. This puts a period at the end of a sentence and begins the next sentence with a capital letter any time you tap the spacebar twice while typing. Tap in the Automatic Full Stop box to turn on the option. See Figure 2-10.

   ■ Auto-capitalization. This feature begins any new sentence with a capital letter.

   ■ Predictive text. The tablet guesses the words you are typing. Some users love this feature; I find it intrusive. Turn it on by tapping in the Predictive Text box. Experiment and see if it makes things easier for you.

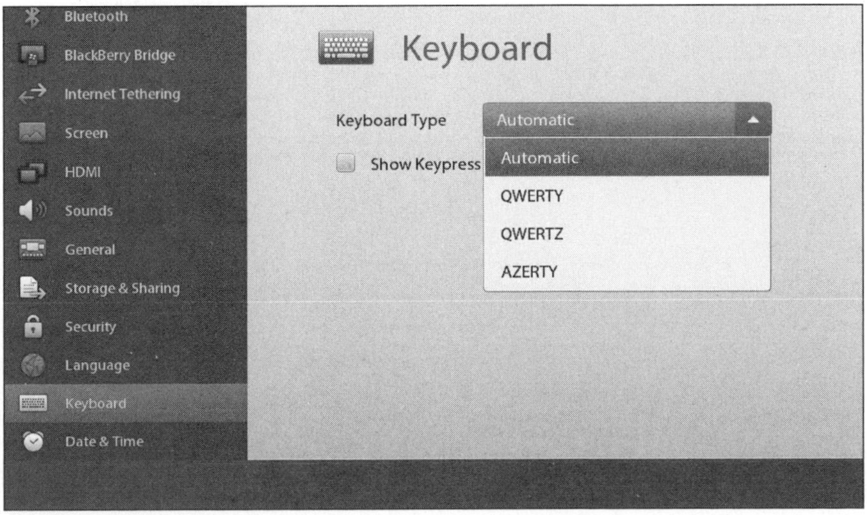

Figure 2-9

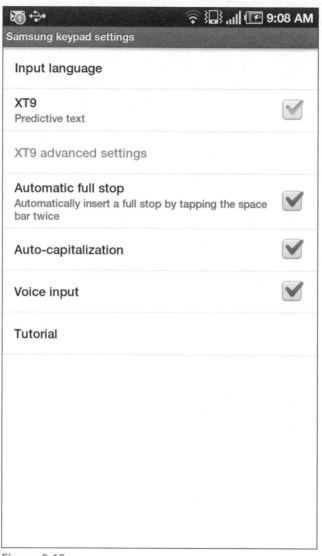

Figure 2-10

Chapter 3

Connecting to the Internet and Other Systems

Y ou can't do much with your tablet without connecting to a network. Without an Internet connection, you can consult the calendar that came with the tablet. Play one of the games that came on it. Take photos or videos. But you expect to be able to read your email. You want to search the web for news or shoes. Use your tablet as a portable video screen or music player. You need an Internet connection to do those things.

tech ₂ to connect

activities

- **Task 1: Using WiFi**
- **Task 2: Using a Cellular Data Network**
- **Task 3: Sharing by Bluetooth**
- **Task 4: Using a Tablet as a Phone**
- **Task 5: Tethering a Tablet**
- **Task 6: Side Loading Files by USB**
- **Task 7: Side Loading Files by Bluetooth**
- **Task 8: Side Loading with a Memory Card**

Task 1: Using WiFi

WiFi is what lets you use a computer network without wires. The Internet is not the same thing as WiFi. WiFi is generally free or inexpensive, and faster than cellular data signals. However, WiFi signals cover only a small area. You may need to hunt for and get close to a strong signal in order to use it.

There are two basic types of WiFi. An open system is for anyone who can get the signal, such as a restaurant or business that has decided to use free and unfettered access to the Internet as a way to attract more visitors. A protected system is for people who pay (like when you buy a muffin at the coffeehouse and they let you use their WiFi). To use a protected system, you have to get a password from the provider (the person who sold you the muffin). Or you may be somewhere that charges — by the minute, hour, or day — to use their wireless connection to the Internet.

Here's how to use WiFi on your tablet:

1. Turn on the WiFi system. On most tablets, this means tapping the settings or data icon and then choosing On. On some tablets, tap the email or Web icon; then your tablet may ask if you want to turn on the WiFi radio. Say yes!

2. Explore the options for setting up WiFi. See Figure 3-1. On many tablets you can ask to be notified any time it finds a signal. You may be able to say that you only want to be informed if the signal is open (does not require a password).

3. Go back to the setup screen. Choose a WiFi network from the list. On most tablets, the best signal is first. Below the name of the system, it says whether it is open or protected. Go to step 4 if you chose an open network. Go to step 5 if you chose a protected network.

4. If you tapped an open network, your tablet will try to connect. If it works, it says Connected. See Figure 3-2. Close the control panel and then tap Web or Email to begin using the Internet. When you are connected to a WiFi signal, you will see an indicator or the word WiFi on the home screen.

5. If you tapped a protected network, you may see a page where you have to enter a password (or a credit card number for billing). If you don't see the page, close the control panel and tap Web.

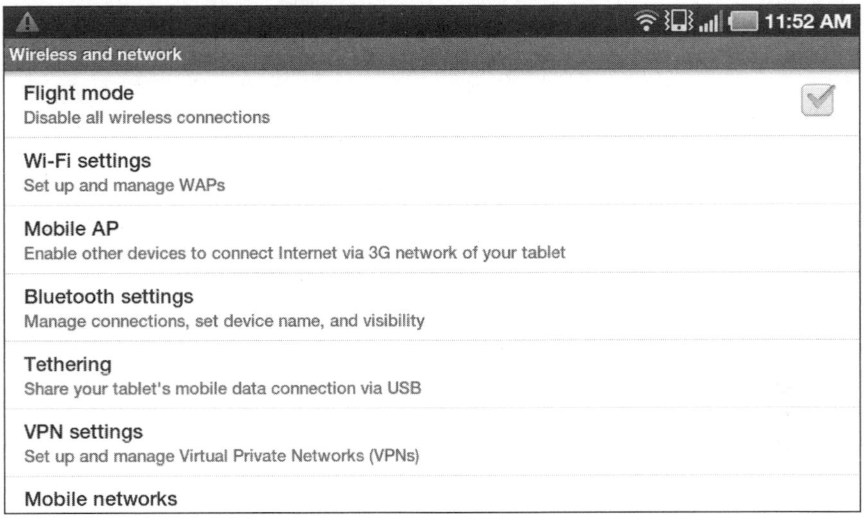

Figure 3-1

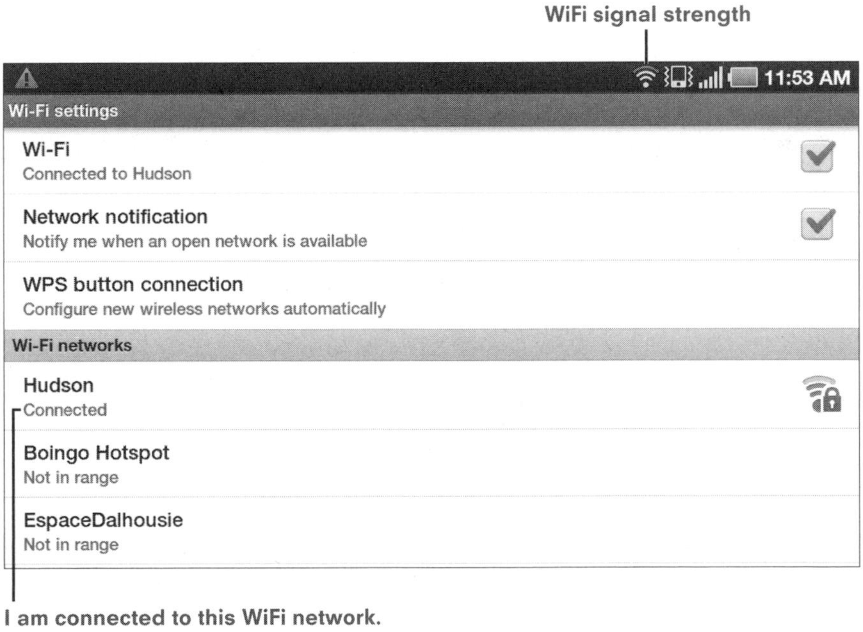

WiFi signal strength

I am connected to this WiFi network.

Figure 3-2

On many tablets you can make it so the password appears on your screen as you enter it, or is shown as ****. Hiding the display of your password may be helpful if you are concerned about someone looking over your shoulder.

Homing in on a WiFi network

WiFi networks are just about everywhere: offices, hotels, libraries, cafés, and private homes. How can you find a WiFi system to use with your tablet? Tap the WiFi app on your tablet's home screen. Move around and watch as the signal strengths change. Move in the direction of the strongest available signal. The icon pointed out in Figure 3-2 shows you the signal strength.

Task 2: Using a Cellular Data Network

Some tablets can connect to the Internet and email by using a cellular data network (instead of WiFi). That is the same system used by smartphones, like the Apple iPhone and various BlackBerry models. If your tablet is a WiFi-only model, it cannot connect to a cellular data network.

A cellular data network has signals almost anywhere you go. Think of how easy it is to whip out a cellphone and make a call from almost anywhere. However, you must pay for a cellular data account with a company (a provider) like T-Mobile or Verizon. Some plans, especially those for roaming (using your tablet outside a particular area) can be pretty expensive. See Figure 3-3 for the kind of warning you might get if you are trying to roam.

⚠ Attention

Allow data roaming? You may incur significant roaming charges!

| Yes | Cancel |

Figure 3-3

Before you use your tablet on a cellular network, have a detailed discussion with your potential provider company's customer service department. Make notes on any prices and promises made. Get a confirmation number or the agent's name. And don't hesitate to call the company every few months to see if any policies have changed or if there are new plans.

Here's how to use a tablet with a cellular data network:

1. Make sure your tablet can use a cellular network (usually 3G or 4G).
2. Get a contract with a cellular provider. On most tablets you can subscribe to a monthly service (for a specific amount of data transfer), or you can use a prepaid plan (and pay for the actual data amount each month).
3. Turn on the cellular data communication system. On most tablets, this means tapping the settings or data icon and then choosing On. On some tablets, if you tap the email or Web icon, your tablet may ask if you want to turn on the cellular data radio. Tap Yes. When you're connected to a cellular signal, an icon or the provider name appears on the home screen.

Turn off the cellular data system after you have finished using it. Some applications may continue communicating (and inflating your bill). And to avoid unpleasant billing surprises, turn off roaming options in the communication setup panel. To turn off your tablet's radio used to communicate with sometimes costly cellular systems, find the Mobile Networks or Cellular Network menu and disable that function. Figure 3-4 shows the Wireless and Network menu on a Samsung Galaxy Tab.

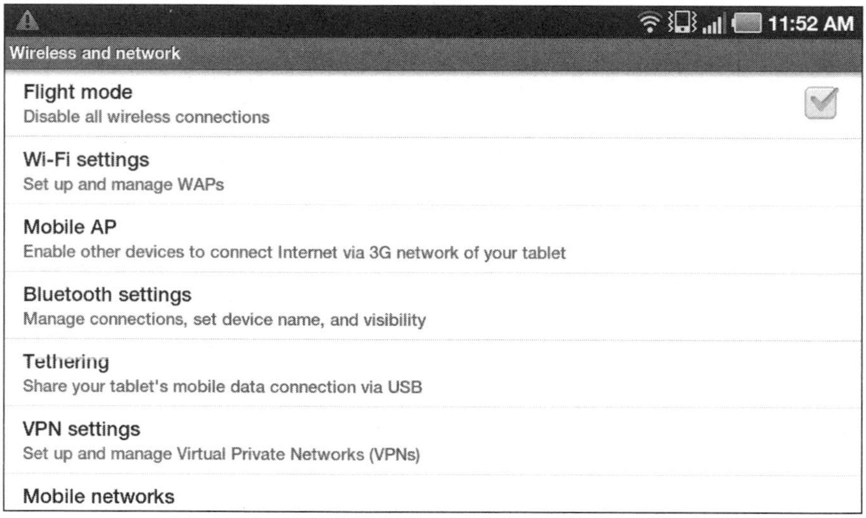

⚠	📶 📳 ▂▄▇ 🔋 11:52 AM
Wireless and network	
Flight mode Disable all wireless connections	☑
Wi-Fi settings Set up and manage WAPs	
Mobile AP Enable other devices to connect Internet via 3G network of your tablet	
Bluetooth settings Manage connections, set device name, and visibility	
Tethering Share your tablet's mobile data connection via USB	
VPN settings Set up and manage Virtual Private Networks (VPNs)	
Mobile networks	

Figure 3-4

Task 3: Sharing by Bluetooth

Bluetooth is another form of wireless communication — like WiFi or cellular radio — but is just for closeup exchanges, like across a room. Nearly all tablets have Bluetooth.

Read the instruction manual for your tablet and the help screens for your desktop computer (or for a plug-in Bluetooth adapter that you might have added to your PC) to learn the specific steps for pairing devices.

Here are the general steps:

1. Turn on your tablet and tap the settings icon (or go to a communication panel). Turn on the Bluetooth radio.
2. Turn on your smartphone, desktop computer, or laptop computer. Go to its communication control panel or special Bluetooth utility that you have installed. Make sure the radio is turned on.
3. Make sure the device is "visible" to other devices. See Figure 3-5.
4. From the tablet's Bluetooth panel, turn on Scan Devices (or a similar command). See Figure 3-6.

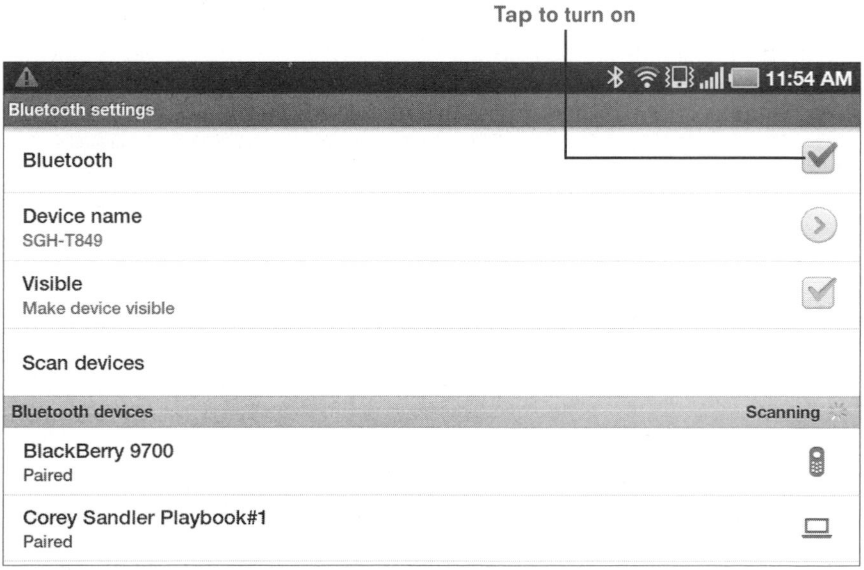

Tap to turn on

Figure 3-5

5. Depending on your tablet, you may have to enter a code. That code is in your tablet's instruction manual. Or, you may have to respond to a message on your tablet, your computer, or both.

6. Do tasks like this:

   ■ Send and receive text, music, or video files from one device to the other.

   ■ Attach and use a gadget such as a physical keyboard, mouse, headset, projector, or speaker.

7. When you are done, turn off or disable the Bluetooth radio from the tablet's control panel. Keep it off until you need it.

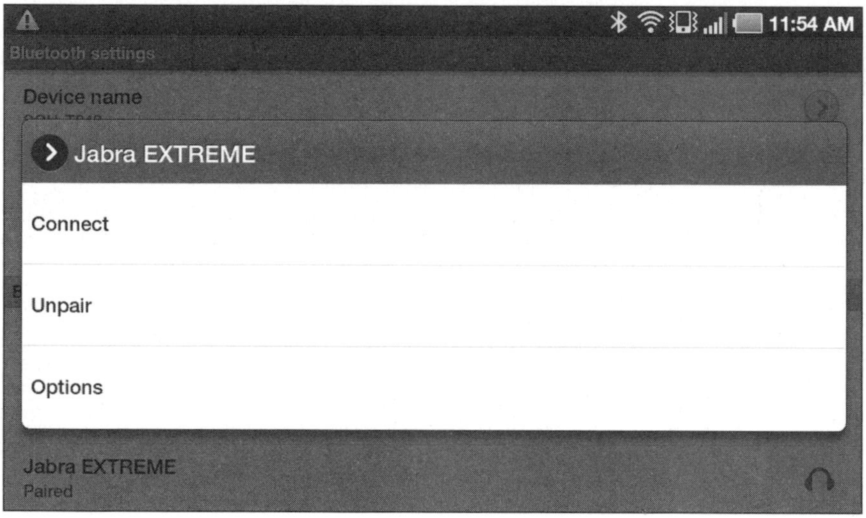

Figure 3-6

Task 4: Using a Tablet as a Phone

Making a phone call using WiFi is usually free or inexpensive. Making a phone call using a cellular data signal may or may not make economic sense. The phone call itself will be cheap, but the roaming charge may be outrageous. To make or receive a phone call, your tablet must be on, and its WiFi connected, and the phone app loaded.

If your tablet offers cellular data connection, contact your cellular provider and learn the full cost of roaming before you make a call.

Here's how to use your tablet as a phone:

1. Enable WiFi (or the cellular data radio) on your tablet and connect to a network. Most tablets use WiFi if it is available, using the slower, more expensive cellular connection only when necessary (and only if you have enabled that feature). If you're not sure whether your tablet will try WiFi first, turn off the cellular data connection when you don't want it to be available.

2. Download and install a telephone application. You can get it from the app store for your tablet or directly from the provider. The app is usually free. Chapter 12 explains how to download an app.

3. Tap the app and follow instructions to set up an account. Depending on the service, you can deposit money to pay for calls or set up a monthly or annual contract. You need to provide a credit card number for payment.

4. Give your phone number to those people who should be able to call you. The provider company will give you the number.

5. Set up a contacts list and tap a name to make a call, or tap the number. See Figure 3-7. Talk into the tablet's built-in microphone. Depending on your tablet, you can plug in a headset (which can help decrease the echo).

Figure 3-7

Task 5: Tethering a Tablet

Tethering can save you the cost of adding a tablet to a cellular data plan. Tethering connects your tablet to your smartphone to use the phone's link to the Internet. Before you tether your tablet to a smartphone, check with customer service at your cellular provider and find out if this is permitted, and if it costs money. Be sure you also understand the pricing. Here are the general steps:

1. Turn on the Bluetooth in your tablet and on your smartphone.
2. Allow the two devices to pair with each other. (Or, on some tablets, connect the smartphone and the tablet using the provided USB cable and select Tethering. You may have to turn off the tablet's WiFi radio.)
3. Turn on the cellular radio in the smartphone and connect to the Internet. Using a cellular data service while roaming may be very costly. Some devices, including most Android-based tablets, also require you to allow tethering in the control panel of the communications, Bluetooth, or other similar menus.
4. On your tablet, tap an icon called Tether or something similar. It may be on the home screen or in a submenu of communication tools. See Figure 3-8.
5. Tap Web, or Browser, or Email, or other such apps.

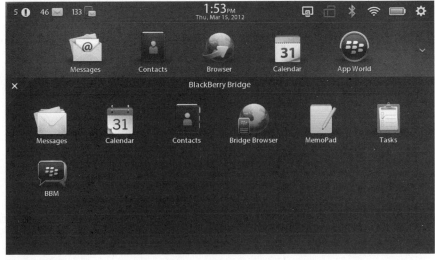

Figure 3-8

Task 6: Side Loading Files by USB

When you download a file, you are requesting it from a source somewhere out there on the Internet and storing a copy on your computer. To upload a file is to go the other way: You send a file (a document or a photo or a song) from your device to the Internet. There, it lives on a site like YouTube, or perhaps you sent it as an email. But what is side loading? It means moving a file from one device to another without the use of the World Wide Web. The source is likely to be a desktop or laptop computer, but it could be tablet or a smartphone.

The specifics of side loading a file to a tablet vary only slightly from one device to another. Here are the basics for a USB cable transfer:

1. Turn on the desktop or laptop computer that has the source files. Allow it to fully load.
2. Open the folder that has the files you want to transfer.
3. Turn on your tablet and allow it to fully load.
4. Attach the USB cable that came with your tablet to the plug (called a port) on that device; connect the other, larger end to a USB port on the desktop or laptop computer. See Figure 3-9. Allow the computer to recognize the presence of the tablet.
5. Tap OK or Yes to let your tablet mount the device.
   - If you have Windows, click Open Folder to View Files (or Open Device to View Files).
   - If you have a Macintosh, a removable drive icon will appear on the desktop. The drive may be labeled with something recognizable (PlayBook or Galaxy, for example) or it may be called something generic or nondescript (External Drive, or NONAME). You can click a drive icon and change its name if that helps you identify it.
6. Find and open the folder for the tablet. Find the files you want to copy to the tablet.
7. Click and drag the icon for the file from its folder on your computer to the folder for your tablet. Put the file in the tablet subfolder it should go in. For example, put video files in the subfolder called Video.
8. Unmount the tablet. Your computer (or smartphone or source tablet) instruction manual has specifics. You may need to tap Unmount or Eject, or right-click with the mouse and choose Eject. Macintosh users can drag the icon for the device to the Trash.
9. Disconnect the USB cable from the file source and then disconnect the cable from the tablet itself.

Plug into
tablet

Plug into desktop
or laptop computer

Figure 3-9

Task 7: Side Loading Files by Bluetooth

If your tablet has Bluetooth, you can use it to side load files. Earlier in this chapter, in "Sharing by Bluetooth," I explain how to set up a Bluetooth link for tasks like tethering a tablet to a smartphone to use the phone's cellular data link to connect to the Internet.

Here, I assume that you have already followed those instructions.

1. Turn on your tablet and go to settings (or to a communication panel).
2. Turn on Bluetooth. Your tablet and computer should automatically connect. If not, you'll see something like Figure 3-10.
3. Follow the instructions for your tablet to transfer files. In most designs, a special Bluetooth menu offers this option.
4. Go through the folders to find the file you want to copy. Tap and follow menu instructions if you are working on the tablet.
5. Tap Yes if you are asked to confirm the transfer.

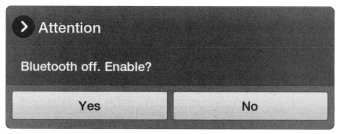

Figure 3-10

Task 8: Side Loading with a Memory Card

Most (but not all) tablets have a slot for a memory card. Read your tablet's instruction manual to learn exactly what you need. There are, amongst others, SD and SDHC designs, and the most commonly used format is the fingernail-sized micro size.

And you may also need to buy a memory card reader for your desktop or laptop computer. Be sure that the reader has a slot for a microSD or microSDHC card if that is what your tablet uses. (Some laptop computers come with a slot for memory cards.)

Most times, I recommend buying a 16GB or 32GB microSDHC card of Class 6 speed. I also suggest buying a brand like Kingston, Lexar, Sandisk, or Transcend. They are more likely to offer a quality product and a warranty. See an example of a memory card in Figure 3-11.

Figure 3-11

Here is how to add files to a memory card from a desktop or laptop computer:

1. Turn off your tablet.
2. Find the slot that holds the memory card; it is usually on one of the four sides, although some have it in a compartment on the back, like the one in Figure 3-12.

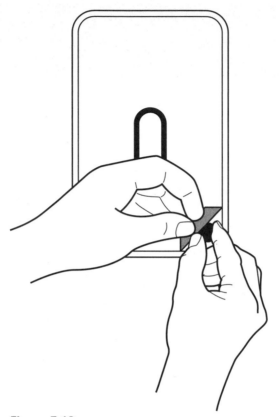

Figure 3-12

3. Carefully remove or open the cover to the slot. (Consult your tablet's instruction manual for details.)

4. Gently pull the card out of its slot. Do not pinch, bend, or compress the card; it should come out with a firm tug. Do not touch the gold contacts on the bottom of the card.

5. Insert the memory card into the reader on your desktop or laptop computer; the device can already be on.

6. Putting the gold contacts in first, gently slide the memory card into place. The memory card will not go in upside down; if it does not slide in place easily, turn it over.

7. On a Windows computer, click Open Folder to View Files (or Open Device to View Files). On a Macintosh system, a removable drive icon will appear on the desktop. The drive may be labeled with something recognizable (PlayBook or Galaxy, for example) or it may be called something generic or nondescript (External Drive, or NONAME). You can click a drive icon and change its name if that helps you identify it.

8. Click and drag the icon for the files you want to copy to the memory card. Put files in the memory card subfolder meant for them. For example, put video files in the folder called Video.

9. Properly eject the card. Your computer (or smartphone or source tablet) instruction manual has specifics. You may need to click Unmount or Eject, or right-click with the mouse and choose Eject. Macintosh users can drag the icon for the device to the Trash.

10. Remove the memory card from the reader attached to (or in) the desktop or laptop computer.

11. Bring the card to your tablet and carefully put it back in its slot.

12. Turn on your tablet. Find videos by tapping the video application, music by tapping a music app, and so on. Or, on most tablets, go to the My Files (or My Stuff) app and see what is on the memory card. Tap a file name to open it.

Chapter 4

Using Email

Back when I was young, I was very much impressed with the U.S. Post Office. Its (unofficial) motto, chiseled into the stone of its downtown station in New York, quoted the ancient Greek historian Herodotus: "Neither snow, nor rain, nor heat, nor gloom of night, stays these couriers from the swift completion of their appointed rounds."

Wow, how time flies. Today many people expect communications to absolutely, positively be there close to instantly. Email can do that.

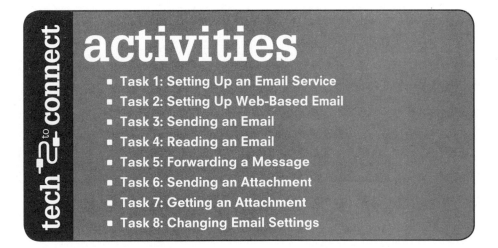

tech 2 to connect

activities

- Task 1: Setting Up an Email Service
- Task 2: Setting Up Web-Based Email
- Task 3: Sending an Email
- Task 4: Reading an Email
- Task 5: Forwarding a Message
- Task 6: Sending an Attachment
- Task 7: Getting an Attachment
- Task 8: Changing Email Settings

Task 1: Setting Up an Email Service

You can get email from a company (like AT&T or Comcast or SBC) or from a web-based service (like Google or Hotmail or Yahoo!). This section explains how to set up an email account with the former. The next section, "Task 2: Setting Up Web-Based Email," explains how to set up the latter.

Your tablet probably came to you with an email app. That is not the same as having email service set up. The email app on your tablet can (probably) work with any service where you set up an account. If you buy Internet access from your local phone or cable television company, or directly from an Internet service provider (ISP), your email address will look something like this: *yourname@serviceprovider*.com. See Figure 4-1.

The steps for setting up an email app are about the same on any tablet. Make sure you have the following written down:

- Email address
- Password
- Incoming mail server
- Outgoing mail server
- Type of server that your provider uses

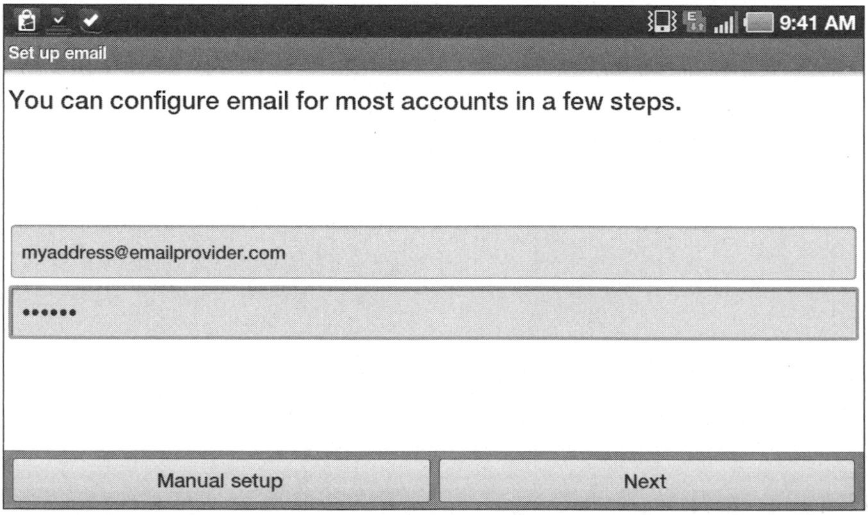

Set up email

You can configure email for most accounts in a few steps.

| myaddress@emailprovider.com |
| ••••••• |

| Manual setup | Next |

Figure 4-1

If you don't know this information, you can find it by clicking the Accounts tab on your personal or laptop computer (if email goes there). Or, call your email or Internet provider.

Here's a general guide to adding an email service to a tablet:

1. Tap the Mail icon on your tablet's home screen. If it's the first time you've tapped it, it might automatically decide that you must want to add an email account. If it doesn't happen automatically, tap the Adding or Configuring an Account button or menu.

2. Tap the Add Account (or similarly named) button.

3. Tap the button labeled Other (or something else non-specific).

4. Type the following information:
   - An account or user name. "My main account," for example, or "My backup account." See Figure 4-2.
   - The email address you use for the account.
   - The password for the account.
   - The type of mail server. The majority use either POP3 or IMAP. You don't have to know anything more than which one they use, but if you drop me an email I will explain more than you need to know.
   - Incoming mail server. On a POP3 server, this might be something like pop.providername.com or mail.providername.com. If your provider uses IMAP, it just might well be something like imap.providername.com.
   - Outgoing mail server. Usually something like smtp.providername.com.

5. Tap the check boxes for other questions. Make sure Delete Email from Server is checked. That gives you a measure of protection for important messages.

6. If you see an option to Require Password for Outgoing Email, leave the option blank. If you encounter a failure, go back and tap this option.

7. If you are creating more than one account, tap Default or Main Account. This tells the tablet which email account to use as the standard.

8. If you see questions you do not understand, you have two choices:
   - Experiment. You can always change your options.
   - Call your email provider or ISP.

9. Tap Done (or Finish or a similarly named command).

10. Immediately send yourself a message from the tablet. Or, even better, send a message from your desktop or laptop computer.

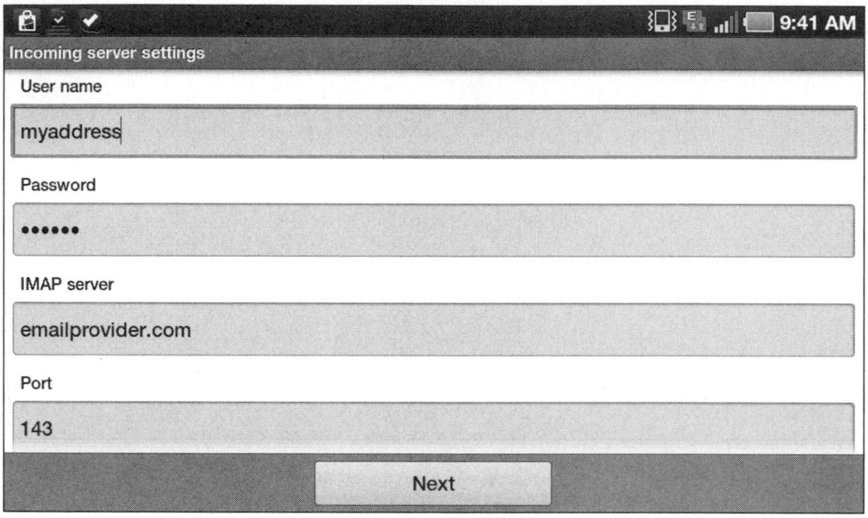

Figure 4-2

Conspiracy theories

I don't want to sound like a paranoid conspiracy theorist here, but you cannot assume that your emails are completely private.

Task 2: Setting Up Web-Based Email

A web-based email service is separate from the company that you pay to get on the Internet. Providers like Google with its Gmail, Yahoo!, AOL, and many others offer free accounts and addresses. Those companies make money from advertisers. You may see ads at the end of email messages that you send or get.

Setting up web-based email service on your tablet may be partially automatic.

1. Tap the Mail icon on your tablet's home screen.
2. Tap the Add Account (or similarly named) button. See Figure 4-3.
3. Find and tap the icon for the web-based email service you use.
4. Type the following information:
   - An account name. "My main account," for example, or "My backup account."
   - The email address you use for the account.
   - The password for the account.
5. Tap Done (or Finish or a similarly named command).

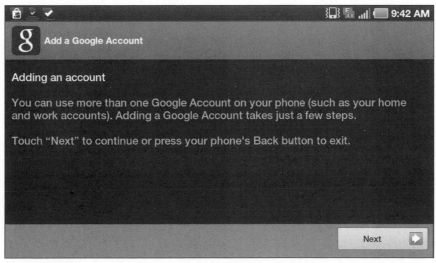

Figure 4-3

Google rules

The Android operating system is a product of the great and powerful Google, so nearly all Android-based tablets will offer a special app just for setting up Gmail. Other manufacturers may strike deals with different email providers, which can mean special icons of that sort on your tablet's home screen.

Task 3: Sending an Email

Once you've got your tablet set up for email, the basic act of sending an email is about as simple as you could hope for.

Here's how to send a simple bit of prose by electronic means:

1. Tap the Mail icon on your tablet's home screen.
2. Make sure you are viewing the inbox. See Figure 4-4 for an example of an inbox. If you are seeing another folder (like Outbox or Sent Messages), simply tap the Inbox label.

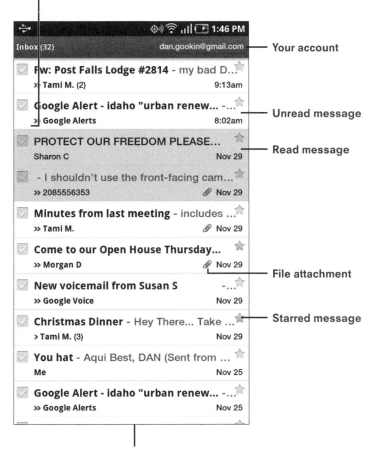

Figure 4-4

3. Tap Compose (or Create Mail, or Write, or a similar verb). If you have more than one account in the same listing, make sure the Sender or From line shows the account you want. If you need to select a different sending account, tap in the Sender or From box and tap the proper source.

4. Tap in the To box. If you have added names and email addresses to your contacts list (more on that later in this chapter), type in the first few letters of the person to whom you want to send email. Tap the option you want. If you want to send an email to someone not in your contacts list, type the complete email address in the To box. Remember, a full address consists of a name, the @ symbol, and the domain name. Something like mybestfriend@heraddress.com.

5. Tap the Subject box and type a subject for the message. It's a good habit to send messages with a subject.

6. Tap in the body of the message. See Figure 4-5. Some email programs automatically look for <u>mispeled</u> <u>werds</u>. Most email programs will let you type a message and save it as a draft. In that case, the message is saved in the Outbox or Pending box. The message, of course, stays where it is until you use the Internet.

7. Tap the Send button. A copy of the message goes into your email program's Sent or Sent Items folder.

If you are using a web-based email service (such as AOL, Gmail, Hotmail, or Yahoo! Mail), and your tablet has an app just for that service, use it. Don't use the other mail app that is on your tablet.

Your email app will have a contacts list — the modern-day equivalent to an address book or a Rolodex. You can fill out the list with names, email addresses, phone numbers, text or instant message addresses, and street addresses. In most cases, tapping an email address opens the mail app and puts that address in the To field. Some tablets do the same with instant messaging addresses.

Here's how to start an email message from the contacts list:

1. Tap the contacts (or people or address book) icon. You can see some of my contacts in Figure 4-6.

2. Type in the person's name. Or, tap the Rolodex-like alphabet listing and tap the exact match.

3. Tap the email address.
    - On some tablets, you end up in a blank email message.
    - On some tablets, you see options including Send Email.
    - On some tablets, you must tap the Menu or Options button and then tap Send Email.

4. Tap the Subject box and type a subject for the message.

5. Tap in the body and type your message.

6. Tap the Send button. A copy of the message goes into your email program's Sent or Sent Items folder.

Figure 4-5

Figure 4-6

Task 4: Reading an Email

The basics of reading email are the same on all tablets. The view will vary depending on your settings and how you are holding the tablet (tall or sideways).

Beside the Inbox on most tablets you will see a number telling you the number of unread messages. On most tablets, unopened email messages show up in bold or colored type, or with a circle or other icon alongside. The mark disappears when you open a message. Remember that you need a live connection to the Internet (by WiFi or by cellular link) to get and send email messages.

To read your mail, do this:

1. Tap the Mail icon on your tablet's home screen. If you have a web-based email service (such as AOL, Gmail, or Hotmail), and your tablet has an app just for that service, tap that icon.

2. Tap a message to read it.

3. Tap Reply to respond to a message. You can see the Reply button in Figure 4-7. To delete a message, tap the Delete button.

4. Tap Send.

Some day you're going to thank me for this: Be very careful before you choose Reply All (instead of Reply). You may not know or see all of the names — all of whom will get your reply. You may miss the name of your boss or your best friend or worst enemy or anyone else you probably do not want to see your response. Only use Reply All after you have duly considered all of the potential consequences and studied all of the addresses to which your response will be sent.

I like my mailbox tidy. How about you?

1. Tap the menu.

2. Type a name for the folder.

3. Tap a message that you want to put in a folder.

4. Tap the Move button.

5. Tap the folder you want the message to go into.

If you have an Apple iPad, you have to do this tidying on your laptop or desktop computer. Any folder you create there will also appear on the matching account that appears on an iPad.

You can easily get to messages that are in folders:

1. Tap the folder name.
2. Tap the message you want to read. Or, you can delete it or reply to it.

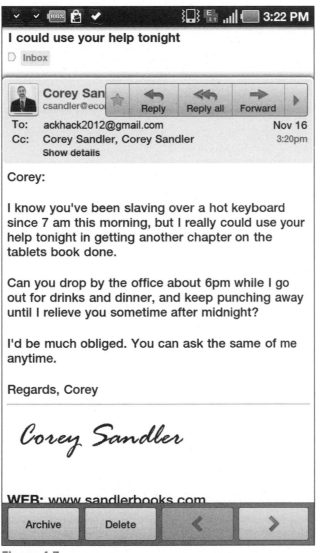

Figure 4-7

Task 5: Forwarding a Message

Forwarding a message sends a copy of an email you have received to another address. When you choose Forward, the Subject box just adds Fwd to the original subject. A forwarded email message will include the name of the original sender, the date and time it was sent, and the email addresses of the senders and recipients.

Here's how to forward an email:

1. Open a message in your mail program.
2. Tap the Forward button. On some tablets you have to tap a menu to find the Forward button.
3. Tap in the To box and type the email address. Or, tap in the To box and start typing the name of someone who is in your contacts list. Tap from the options that appear.
4. Decide if you want to use the available options. Many email programs offer Quoted Text or Respond Inline. Here's what those options mean:
   - Quoted Text sends the entire original message in your new message. In general, you cannot change the forwarded message. Tap in the message box to type a note.
   - Respond Inline (or Reply Inline) sends the original email in the message box. You can tap in the original message to change it. See Figure 4-8.
5. Tap Send.

Read the entire message before you forward it. Do you really want all recipients to know all of the information it contains? Are you possibly violating someone's expectation of privacy by passing along all email addresses? Remember, too, that a recipient of a forwarded message might choose to forward it to a new group of people, spreading its contents (and email addresses) to persons you have not chosen.

Figure 4-8

Task 6: Sending an Attachment

Can you remember your first attachment? The thrill of victory, the agony of defeat. Enough about high school. Let's talk about our mature, modern lives. A time when we use our high-tech tablets to send photographs of the kids and grandchildren, video clips of cats stuck in shoe boxes, and singing birthday cards. Most of those are sent as attachments to emails, which means you are passing along a separate file with the email message.

It's easy to attach a file to an email. And it's usually easy to play or display an attachment you receive. But some types of files cannot be sent or accepted.

Here's how to add an attachment — a text document, photo, video, or audio recording — to an email:

1. Tap the mail app icon. If you have a web-based email service (such as AOL, Gmail, Hotmail, or Yahoo! Mail), and your tablet has an app just for that service, tap that icon.

2. Create a message by choosing a recipient, adding a subject, and tapping in a bit of text. Details are in this chapter's earlier section, "Sending an Email."

3. Tap the Attachments button. Sometimes the button is shown as a paper clip. On the Samsung Galaxy Tab, press the menu button on the tablet's frame (not the menu icon on the screen). The menu button looks like what you see to the left.

4. Tap the Attach button. See Figure 4-9.

5. Tap Browse and look for the file.

6. Tap the file you want to send when you find it.

7. Tap Open or Attach.

8. Tap Send. You may have to tap a menu to see the Send option.

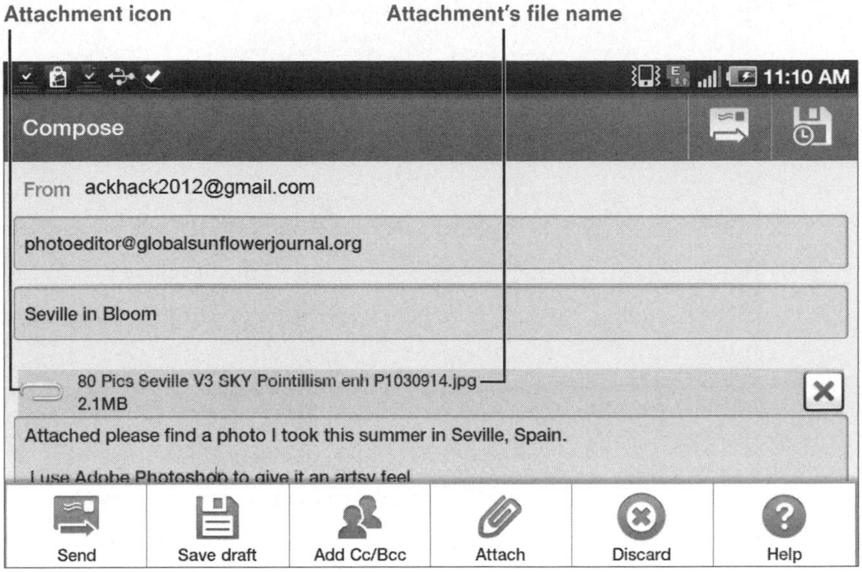

Attachment icon   Attachment's file name

Figure 4-9

You can also send an attachment another way. Start the app that has the file you want to send. For example, if you go to the folder that holds photos you have taken with your tablet (it might be called Photos, Pictures, Gallery, or something like that) and select an image, you can send it over the Internet. Here's how:

1. From the home screen, tap the app that has the file you want to send. Gallery, Pictures, or Photos are likely suspects.

2. Open any subfolder to display a photo you want to send.

3. Tap a picture.

4. Do one of the following, depending on your tablet. Try each one until you find the one that works. It won't hurt the tablet.
   - Press and hold the picture.
   - Touch the menu button (on the frame of the Samsung Galaxy Tab).
   - Tap the menu icon.

5. Tap Share.

6. Tap the email app option. In Figure 4-10, you can see Gmail is an option.

7. Tap in the To box and type a name or email address.

8. Tap in the Subject box and type a subject.

9. Tap in the email body and type a message.

10. Tap Send. You may have to tap a menu to see the Send option.

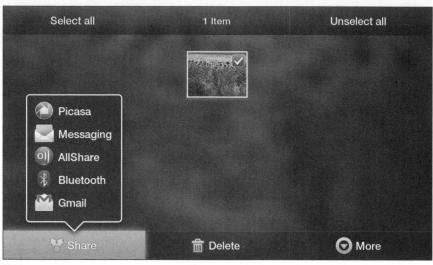

Figure 4-10

Task 7: Getting an Attachment

You don't have to do anything special to receive an attachment: It just comes in with the mail. However, keep three important things in mind:

- Some email services (especially the web-based services like Gmail or Hotmail) may limit how big incoming attachments can be.
- A large incoming attachment will take more time to get to you (and may cost more money if you use a cellular connection to receive it). See Chapter 3 for information about cellular versus WiFi connections.
- You may be able to get an attachment that your tablet can't work with.

Here's how to work with an attachment that arrives on your tablet:

1. Tap the message to open it. The message will have a paper clip icon or have a notice that says attachment. See Figure 4-11.
2. Tap Preview to see what's in the document without leaving the email program.
3. Tap Save. Most tablets save the attachment in the Download folder.

Some email programs tell you if there is a picture included in the message (which is different than it being attached to the message). Some email programs will not show you the picture. Just tap the Show Pictures button (or something named similarly).

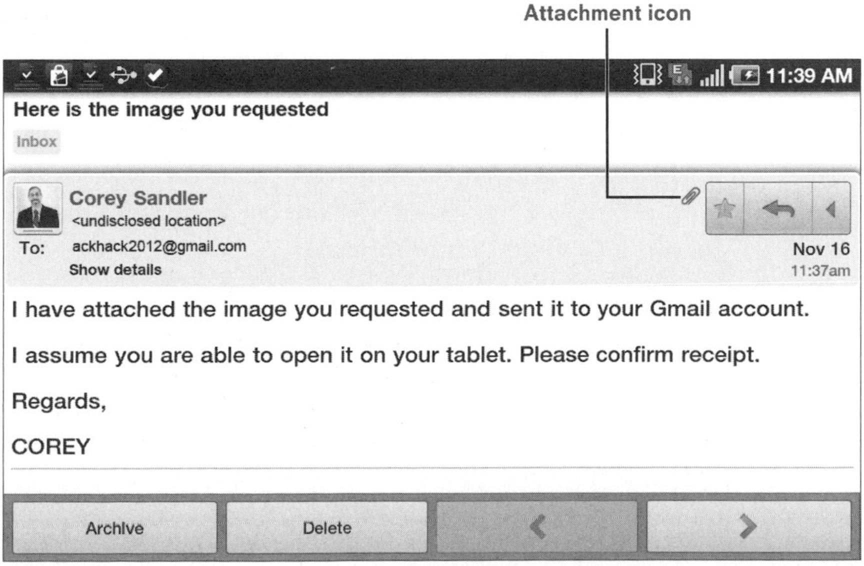

Attachment icon

Figure 4-11

Task 8: Changing Email Settings

You can set up your email program to an extent. Your tablet may have some or all of the features; email programs often change, so if your email service does not have every one of these options today, it might tomorrow.

Here's how to make your email more how you like it:

1. Tap the email icon on your tablet's home screen.
2. Tap the Settings or Option button. You may have to first press the menu key on the tablet's frame, or tap the menu icon on the screen.
3. Tap to decide on the options you find. Some of the more common options are explained here. See Figure 4-12.

   ▪ Set the default email account. If you have more than one email address, this setting tells the tablet which one to use for outgoing messages.

   ▪ Get an alert when a message is successfully sent. If you want, you can hear bells (or a chime) when a message has left your tablet and is winging its way over the Internet to its destination.

   ▪ Get an alert when a message is received. Hear an alert anytime you get a message. If you want to (or need to) be distracted from whatever else you are doing every time a piece of mail arrives, select this option.

   ▪ Add a signature to every message. A signature appends the same text (your name and contact information, for example) to every message you send.

   ▪ Always BCC (blind carbon copy) yourself. You can send a copy of every message to your inbox.

   ▪ Specify the number of messages that show in your Inbox. This does not mean you can't get to any other messages.

   ▪ Set the size of a message preview. The more lines you see, the fewer messages you can see before you have to scroll down. The number of messages and preview lines that can be seen is also affected by whether you choose to hold the tablet upright or sideways.

   ▪ Display images. Not showing an embedded (versus an attached) photo helps the message show on your screen more quickly. More importantly, it may keep certain destructive viruses from getting to your tablet.

   ▪ Adjust the type size in your messages. You might get to choose among small, medium, large, extra large, and giant. Other tablets offer specific point sizes of type; the larger the point size, the larger the characters.

   ▪ Confirm deletion. If you tap Delete, your tablet will ask you again, just to make sure. This can help make sure you don't accidentally delete an email.

   ▪ Determine how often your tablet checks for new email. See Figure 4-13.

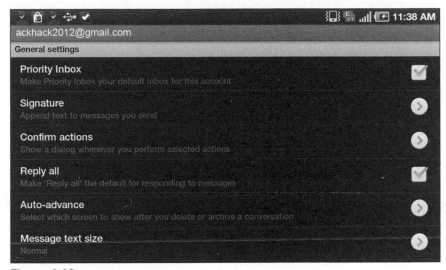

Figure 4-12

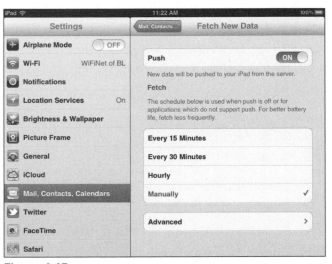

Figure 4-13

Chapter 5

Going Online

Today, people mostly talk about the web, or the Internet. The Internet is very much like the back room off of my office. It's large, full of stuff, and I really don't have much of a clue as to what is stored within it. But I do know that there are some really important and interesting things there. Somewhere.

All tablets have a web browser. Some, like Apple, have a fancy name like Safari. Others just call it what it is: a browser. From your tablet's web browser, you can find all sorts of glorious things on the Internet.

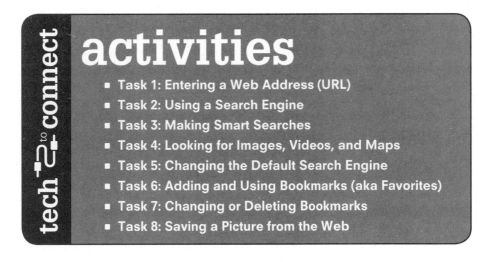

tech to connect

activities

- Task 1: Entering a Web Address (URL)
- Task 2: Using a Search Engine
- Task 3: Making Smart Searches
- Task 4: Looking for Images, Videos, and Maps
- Task 5: Changing the Default Search Engine
- Task 6: Adding and Using Bookmarks (aka Favorites)
- Task 7: Changing or Deleting Bookmarks
- Task 8: Saving a Picture from the Web

Task 1: Entering a Web Address (URL)

Say you want to visit the AARP home page. That just happens to be at `www.aarp.org`. Or perhaps you are curious about my website, which is at `www.sandlerbooks.com`. If you know the specific address for a particular website, you can type it directly into the address bar of the web browser on your tablet.

Here is how to enter a web address into a tablet browser:

1. Tap the icon for the browser. Some tablets show the word Web just below the icon. You might instead see an icon that leads directly to a site on the Internet, such as Google or *The New York Times*. All of them use your tablet's browser.

2. Tap in the address bar. It may be completely blank, or it may have a web address like `http://www.nytimes.com`. Figure 5-1 shows what happens when I tap in my address bar. Your keyboard will appear.

3. Type the address you want to visit. Do not worry about uppercase letters. Apple iPad and BlackBerry PlayBook show sites that you have visited before. To go there, tap the name.

4. Tap Go.

WWW

No one really calls it the *World Wide Web* anymore, although that was one of its original names (and it is the origin of the *www* at the start of a web page). Today, we mostly talk about the *web* or the *Internet* or we might refer to it as *going online*.

Address bar

Figure 5-1

You don't have to type in http or www. Just enter the name and its suffix (`aarp.org` or `sandlerbooks.com`). The system can handle it.

Task 2: Using a Search Engine

A search engine is a piece of software (a program, if you will) that lives on your tablet and lets you hunt for something: a website, a name or address, a photo or video, or anything else. The most famous search engine is Google, followed by Yahoo! and Bing.

Use the search engine that came on your tablet or use the browser to go to `google.com` or `bing.com` or `yahoo.com`.

Here's how to look for something with a search engine:

1. Tap the shortcut on your tablet's home page that takes you directly to a search engine. It may say Web or Browser underneath the icon. See Figure 5-2.
2. Tap in the search bar. Then type in details of what you are looking for.
3. Tap Go.
4. Read through the list and tap the website you want.

Tap this icon. ———

Figure 5-2

Task 3: Making Smart Searches

There are searches and there are smart searches. The more prepared you are, the better your results. You're thinking, "I'd like to see some great plays made in this year's baseball World Series." If you type Series Champions into the search engine, you might get results for the World Series of Poker, the Little League World Series, a Wikipedia article about the history of the World Series, a website selling tickets to the World Series, and a bunch of pages about world peace, world war, Shakespearean plays. Figure 5-3 shows the results I got, in the Google search engine, for Porto Mahon, Spain.

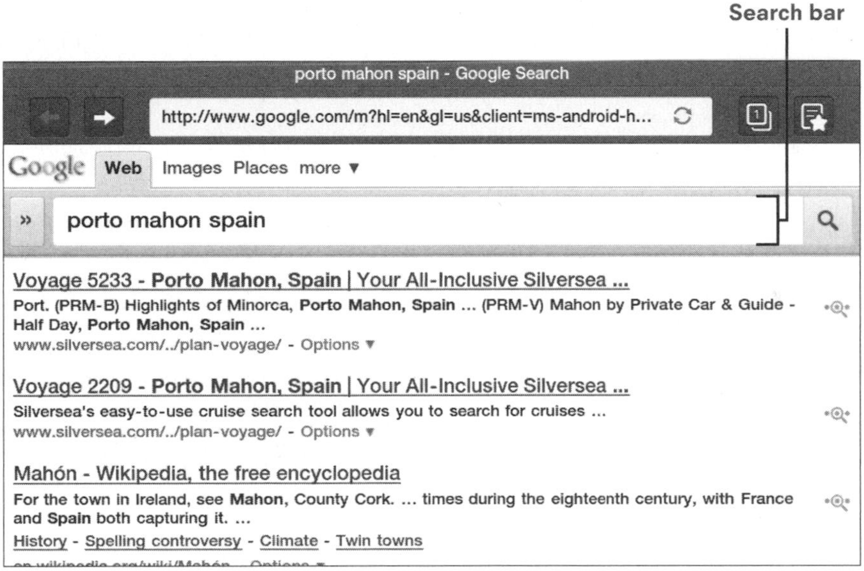

Search bar

Figure 5-3

Don't worry about capital letters unless you are using OR, AND, or NOT.

Improve your searches with these tips:

- Put quotation marks around phrases. Typing "World Series" brings up only results with those two words in that exact order.
- Use OR, AND, and NOT. For example, try *heart OR cardiac*. Including OR means you will get results with either word returned. If you wanted to learn more about surgical procedures related to the human vascular system, you might get better results by searching for *heart OR cardiac*. The inclusion of

OR means that you get results with either word. But say you want to exclude a particular group from your results. Back to baseball: Now exclude poker from your inquiry. In Google, you can use the minus sign to indicate NOT: Try *World Series -poker*. Note that the minus sign goes directly before the word you want to exclude, without a space after the sign.

What in the world is the web?

If you want to pick a nit, the web is just one of the services that is provided over the Internet. There are also things like VOIP (Voice over Internet Protocol) and streaming audio and video services. You can also use one of many social networking programs like Twitter or Facebook.

Task 4: Looking for Images, Videos, and Maps

Most major search engines let you look for things besides words. You can also look for images, videos, maps, and other graphical elements. In Figure 5-4, I typed *porto mahon spain* and clicked the Images tab. These are my results.

Here's how to search for something like a photo or a map or a video:

1. Tap the web browser icon.

2. Type your search query in the address bar. Fine-tune your search if necessary using quote marks, OR, AND, or NOT.

3. When you get results, tap Images, Videos, Maps, Blogs, or Shopping. You may need to tap the word More to see options besides websites. See Figure 5-5.

Click this tab to see images only.

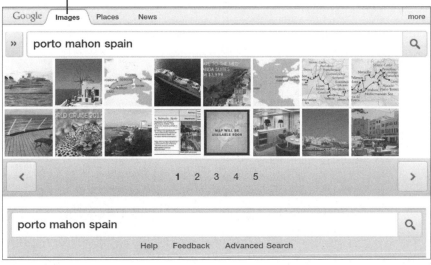

Figure 5-4

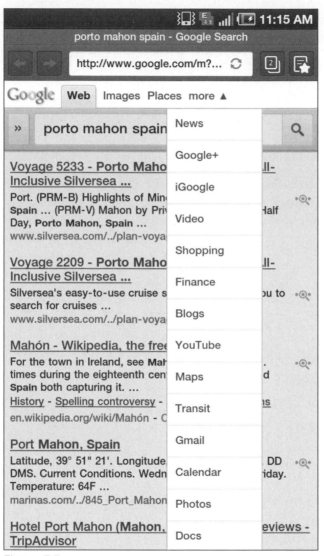

Figure 5-5

Task 5: Changing the Default Search Engine

Your tablet comes to you already with a search engine. Apple iPad and Samsung Galaxy Tab (and many other Android devices) use Google. BlackBerry PlayBook offers Bing. But you don't have to use those search engines. You can make your default engine something else. (The default is the particular search engine your tablet goes to automatically; you can always enter a different web address for a search engine.)

Follow these steps if you have an **Apple iPad**:

1. Go to the home screen.
2. Tap the settings icon, which is pointed out in Figure 5-6.
3. Use your magic finger to move down the list. Tap Safari, the name of the iPad's browser.
4. Tap Search Engine.
5. Tap Bing or Yahoo!

If you use an **Android** tablet, you can probably change the default search engine this way:

1. Tap the web browser icon.
2. Tap the menu button, which is not on the screen. It is on the frame of the device and looks like the icon next to this step.
3. Tap Settings.
4. Go to the Advanced section and tap the option that says Set Search Engine.
5. Scroll through the list and tap your choice.

If your Android tablet does not let you change the search engine this way, follow these steps:

1. Tap the web browser icon.
2. Tap in the address bar and type the engine you want to use.
3. Tap the bookmark icon in the upper-right corner.
4. Tap the search engine that you have added to the favorites list.

If you have a **BlackBerry PlayBook**, change the default search engine this way:

1. Tap the browser or web icon.
2. Swipe down from the top frame of your tablet onto the screen.
3. Tap Options.
4. Tap the General tab.
5. Find the search engine setting. See Figure 5-6.
6. Tap the down-pointing arrow.
7. Tap the choice you want.
8. Tap somewhere outside of the menu.

Settings icon

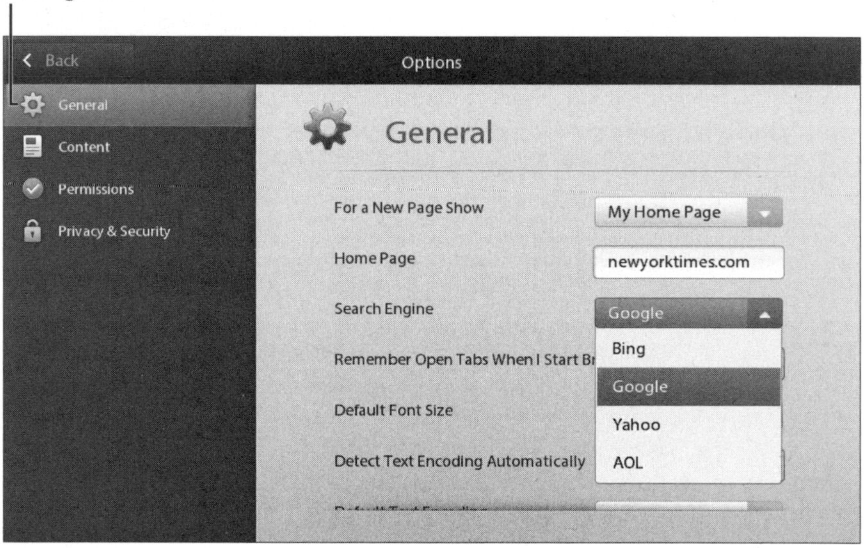

Figure 5-6

Task 6: Adding and Using Bookmarks (aka Favorites)

You can easily place a bookmark that lets you quickly jump to a website at the tap of a finger.

To use a bookmark, follow these steps:

1. Tap the Web browser icon.
2. Tap the bookmark icon. Some look like the one shown in Figure 5-7. Some are stars.
3. Tap the bookmark for the website you want to visit.

Here's how to add a bookmark:

1. Tap the Web browser icon.
2. Tap in the address bar and type where you want to go.
3. When the page appears, tap the add bookmark icon.
4. Follow the rest of the steps depending on what kind of tablet you have.

If you have an **Apple iPad**, follow these steps:

5. Tap Add Bookmark.
6. Tap the X in the circle next to the name or just go to step 8.
7. Type a name for the bookmark.
8. Tap Save.

If you have an **Android** tablet, follow these steps:

5. Tap Bookmarks.
6. Tap in the address bar.
7. Type the web address you want to store as a bookmark.
8. Tap OK.

If you have a **BlackBerry PlayBook**, follow this step:

5. Tap the add bookmark icon in the upper-right corner. The icon is a star with a + sign.

Previous

Next Page

Bookmarks

Go To...

Search Google,
Bing, or Yahoo!

Address field

Reload Web Page

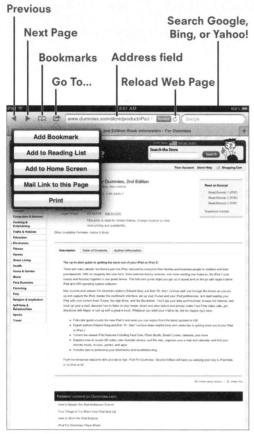

Figure 5-7

Task 7: Changing or Deleting Bookmarks

On Android and Apple iPad tablets, you can edit the bookmark name to whatever you want (or put it wherever you want). Or, you can delete a bookmark altogether. Here's how to delete a bookmark:

1. Tap the Web browser icon.
2. Tap the bookmark icon.
3. Follow the rest of the steps depending on what kind of tablet you have.

If you have an **Apple iPad**, tap the red circle next to the bookmark you want to get rid of. To rename or move it somewhere else, follow these steps:

4. Tap Edit.
5. Tap the X (in the gray circle) in the Name field.
6. Type a new title. If that's all you want to do, go to step 8.
7. Move the bookmark with these options:
   - Tap Edit and drag the three bars (to the right of the bookmark's name) to a new location.
   - Tap the > symbol. Scroll through the list and tap the folder where you want to put the bookmark.
   - Tap Edit and then tap the New Folder button. Type a new folder name and choose where it should go.
8. Tap Save.

If you have a **BlackBerry PlayBook**, follow these steps:

4. Tap the pencil icon (in the upper-right corner of the Bookmark display).
5. Tap the X next to the bookmark you want to delete.

If you have an **Android** tablet, follow these steps:

4. Tap the Edit button in the list of saved websites.
5. Tap the bookmark. You will see something similar to Figure 5-8.
6. Tap in the Title box.
7. Type a new name for the bookmark. Skip to step 10 if you are done.

8. Tap the down-pointing arrow in the Select Folder box if you want to move the bookmark.
9. Tap the folder where you want the bookmark to go.
10. Tap OK.

Figure 5-8

Task 8: Saving a Picture from the Web

Did that cat really get stuck in the oatmeal box? This picture cannot go unshared. But what can you do? Not everything is permanent on the web. A story may be removed after a few days, or the website may not always be available.

Some images may not let you save or copy. However, you can read Chapter 6 to see how to make a screen capture of an entire web page. Also, you cannot save or copy most videos using your tablet. To capture basically means to take a picture of an image, application, or website displayed on the screen of your tablet. There is no camera involved; you are capturing the digital information for what you see on screen.

To capture and store a copy of an image from a website, do this:

1. Tap the web browser icon.
2. Go to a web page that has a picture.
3. Touch your finger to the image and hold it in place for a second or two.
4. Tap Save Image. See Figure 5-9.

Different tablets store the pictures in different places. Apple iPads save them to your Photos library. Android devices save the image to the Gallery folder, in a subfolder called Download. BlackBerry PlayBooks let you type a name for the file and then the image is saved in the Pictures folder, in a subfolder called Downloads.

Who's your lawyer?

I freely look at, comment about, and alert my friends and family to the presence of images posted on the web. However, many images are protected by copyright, which restricts you to certain options. For example, the copyright holder of images on a website might allow you to make copies for your own personal use but usually will be mightily displeased if you then turn around and reuse them for a commercial purpose. Whatever you do, don't sell an image you don't own unless you get written permission (or pay for a license) from its owner.

Figure 5-9

Chapter 6

Taking Pictures

U sing a tablet to take a photograph is a bit like holding up a picture frame to capture an image. Most tablets also include a high-definition video camera, and some also add a kind of flash. Ready? Cheese!

Note that entry-level tablets such as the Amazon Kindle Fire and the Barnes & Noble NOOK Tablet do not have cameras.

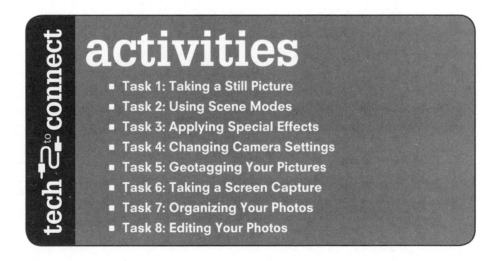

tech to connect

activities

- Task 1: Taking a Still Picture
- Task 2: Using Scene Modes
- Task 3: Applying Special Effects
- Task 4: Changing Camera Settings
- Task 5: Geotagging Your Pictures
- Task 6: Taking a Screen Capture
- Task 7: Organizing Your Photos
- Task 8: Editing Your Photos

Task 1: Taking a Still Picture

You have to make sure the tablet knows it needs to act like a camera, which you do here in Step 1. Pictures that you take are saved in the default folder for pictures.

1. Tap the camera icon. The icon is usually on the home screen.

2. Tap the camera icon. Some tablets have a front-facing and a rear-facing camera. In that case, an icon or an option box is there so you can tell the tablet which way the camera should face. See Figure 6-1.

3. Hold the tablet firmly in front of you with both hands. Frame the image you want to capture. See Figure 6-2.

4. Tap the camera icon to take the picture. (Tap the icon on the picture-taking screen, not the icon on the home screen.) You might hear a picture-taking click.

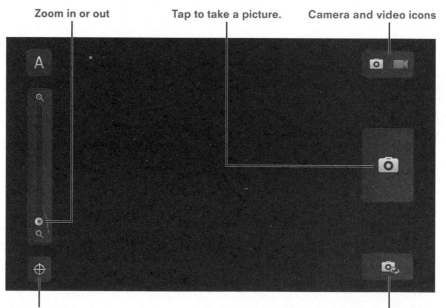

Figure 6-1

Figure 6-2

You can use your tablet as a form of electronic scanner, making copies of receipts and other documents. Lay the paperwork flat on a counter and make sure it is well lit (in direct sunlight or under a task lamp shining directly). Hold your tablet as close to the paperwork as possible.

Task 2: Using Scene Modes

Your tablet can take very good close-up photos (portraits, for example) or landscapes or action shots. Choose a scene mode, available on many tablets, based on what you want to photograph.

Here's how to use scene modes:

1. Tap the camera icon. It is usually on the home screen.
2. Tap the scene icon. It may say Scene or SCN. Look at Figure 6-3 to see an example.
3. Tap one of the modes. Here are some typical offerings:

   - Normal or None. This is the standard setting for the camera. If you are in another mode, tap Normal or None to return to regular picture-taking.
   - Portrait. With this you can take a picture of someone or something pretty close to you (about 3 to 10 feet away). Turn on the flash when you are taking a picture of someone who has the bright light behind them. In this chapter, "Task 4: Changing Camera Settings," tells you how to turn on the flash.
   - Landscape. This mode makes the most of the photographs you take from on top of Old Smoky (or anywhere you want as much of the scene in focus as possible). Camera buffs call this a wide depth of field, meaning objects close to and far from the camera are in focus.
   - Night. This setting allows in as much light as possible, often using a slow shutter speed. The result may be blurring of people or objects in motion.
   - Sports. This setting emphasizes a faster shutter speed to stop action. The downside may be a shorter depth of field: People or objects at a distance from the subject of the picture may be out of focus.

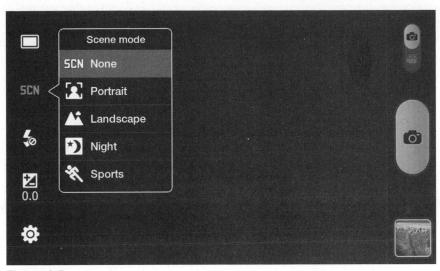

Figure 6-3

Task 3: Applying Special Effects

Because your tablet is a computer, it can perform a wide range of fancy tricks that change a photograph. Here's how:

1. Tap the camera icon. It is usually on the home screen.

2. Tap the options or settings menu. Some tablets have an icon that looks like a gear. On the BlackBerry PlayBook, swipe down from the top frame.

3. Tap an effect. Choose one of these before you take the picture:

   ▪ Negative. The effect is similar to what a color film negative looked like before it was projected onto photographic paper to make a print. How 20th century! See Figure 6-4.

   ▪ Black and white. A retro look, like the old photos rustling around in old albums and high school yearbooks. It can make for a very nice portrait or landscape. See Figure 6-5.

   ▪ Sepia. If you really want to go retro, sepia has shades of dark brown. You can unleash your inner Mathew Brady.

Instead of applying special effects to a picture as you're taking it, consider taking a regular shot without any effects. Then transfer the file to your desktop or laptop computer. (See Chapter 3 for how to do that.) There you can mess around with the picture using something like Adobe Elements or iPhoto Editor. Make a copy of the original full-color file and then apply effects like black-and-white, sepia, or negative.

Figure 6-4

Figure 6-5

Task 4: Changing Camera Settings

The tablet may look like a blank slate, but once again you do have the power to unleash the camera within, in a point-and-shoot kind of way. Most tablets allow you to make adjustments to some of the technical side of digital photography.

To change settings, do this:

1. Tap the camera icon. It is usually on the home screen.
2. Tap the options or settings menu. Some tablets have an icon in the shape of a gear. On the BlackBerry PlayBook, swipe down from the top frame.
3. Choose the settings you want:

   - Resolution. The higher the resolution, the more detail you get. High-resolution pictures have much larger files, which take longer to send over the Internet or side load (copy). You definitely want high resolution if you plan to print an image.
   - Flash. You can turn the flash on or off, or use auto (which lets the tablet decide whether to use the flash). Using the flash uses lots of battery power. To save power, make sure the flash setting is off when you don't need it. See Figure 6-6.
   - Continuous shots. Your tablet camera has shutter lag, which means when you tap the button to take a picture, the tablet waits a second before it snaps the image. Shutter lag is a problem if you're trying to photograph a fidgety baby. Continuous mode fires off a group of photos, one after another. The trick is to start shooting before you see the one you want and hope that somewhere in the middle is a keeper.

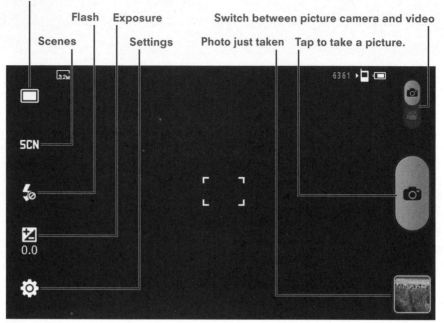

Figure 6-6

Task 5: Geotagging Your Pictures

I'm trying my best to steer clear of technical bafflegab as much as possible, but there is one word you might want to learn. Who knows? You might just impress your kids. Geotagging means attaching a geographic description to an image. The geotag can be latitude and longitude or the actual location.

Consider whether you want to share your physical location — especially if you plan to share your photo on a website like Flickr.

Here's how to use geotagging with your tablet:

1. Tap the camera icon. It is usually on the home screen.
2. Tap the options or settings menu. Some tablets have an icon that looks like a gear. On the BlackBerry PlayBook, swipe down from the top frame.
3. Tap the setting that is named geotagging (or GPS or Location or Show on Map). See Figure 6-7.
4. Tap the option (or move a switch to On, or tap a check mark in a box beside the setting). It may take a while for the tablet to figure out where it is. My geotag is shown in Figure 6-8.

If your tablet uses cellular data, carefully consider whether you want to use geotagging outside of your home region. Roaming can wind up in a very large bill. Using a WiFi connection is often a better choice. Some links are free and open to the public. Read about cellular and WiFi connections in Chapter 3.

Figure 6-7

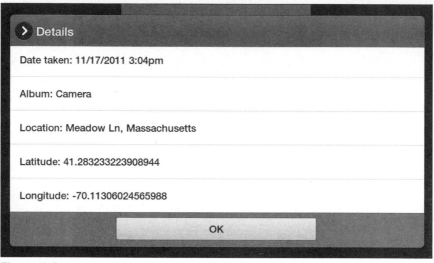

Figure 6-8

Task 6: Taking a Screen Capture

There's one other form of photograph worth noting: a screen capture. You can do the same things with a screen capture that you can do with a photograph: edit it, email it, or print it. For example, snap a capture of a web page as confirmation of an order or a price quote. Capture a still shot from a video or a picture on a travel site. (Or you can take screen captures for use in a book like the one you are reading right now. Figure 6-9 is an example.)

Overall, many sites let you make a copy for your personal use, but you have to get permission from the image's or website's owner before you can use the screen capture for commercial use. And, some screens won't let you take the capture. Always check the sections marked Legal and Terms and Conditions on a website to determine how you can use the content.

If you have a tablet other than the kinds mentioned in this book, read the tablet's manual or go to a search engine on the web and type in this: screen capture on *tablet name*. (Type in the name of your tablet, of course.)

Here's how to take a photograph (a capture) of whatever is showing on your tablet's screen:

1. Make sure that what is on your tablet's screen is what you want to capture.
2. Tap the button. Here are some typical steps:

   - **Apple iPad2.** Hold down the power button and then press the home button (shown to the left). You should see a flash on the screen and hear a click. Go to Photos and check your camera roll to find the screen capture.
   - **BlackBerry PlayBook.** Press the – and + buttons (the volume decrease and increase buttons) on the top edge of the tablet.
   - **Samsung Galaxy Tab.** Hold the back button (shown to the left) and press the power button. You should hear a click. The screen capture is saved in a folder called ScreenCapture.

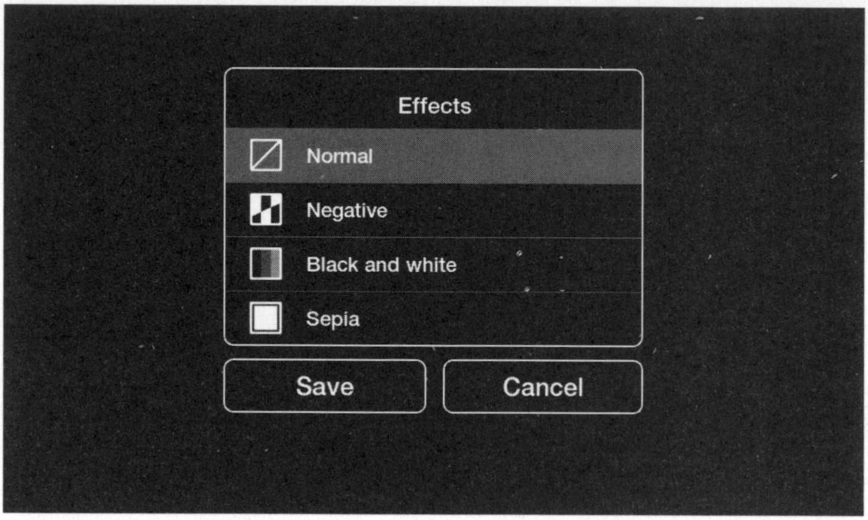

Figure 6-9

Task 7: Organizing Your Photos

It's a good idea to put every photo in a Photo or Image or Media folder, like those you see in Figure 6-10.

Here's how to organize your images:

1. Turn on your tablet.
2. Go to the home screen.
3. Tap the icon called Gallery, Media, Pictures, Images, or something similar. You will then see all the images it can find. See Figure 6-11.

    ■ On the **BlackBerry PlayBook**, swipe down from the top frame to see your choices.

    ■ On an **Android** tablet or an **Apple iPad**, tap the menu button to see your choices. The menu button will look like what you see to the left.

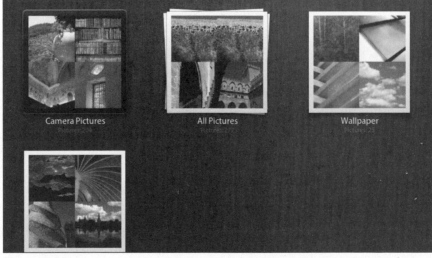

Figure 6-10

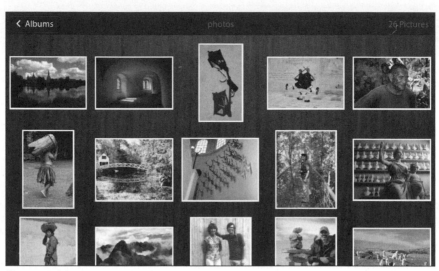

Figure 6-11

Task 8: Editing Your Photos

When your pictures are on a laptop or desktop computer, there are so-called programs that can easily fix things like exposure and color. But what about the photos you take on your tablet? You have two options:

- You can side load the pictures to a desktop or laptop computer. Chapter 3 tells you how to do that. When you're done side loading and editing, you can put the edited picture back on your tablet if you want to.
- You can download and install an image-editing application like the one in Figure 6-12. I tell you how to download and install applications (aka apps) in Chapter 12.

Figure 6-12

Adobe Photoshop Express is an example of a program that edits photographs. If you have an Android or Apple iPad tablet, you can get Adobe Photoshop Express for free.

Here's how to use Adobe Photoshop Express on an Android-based tablet:

1. Tap the icon for the app store. The icon is usually on the home screen, like in Figure 6-13. When you download the app, it will automatically be installed on your tablet.
2. Tap the Photoshop Express app, which will start the program.

3. Tap any image.

4. Edit your picture. The simple tools include exposure, saturation (color intensity), and special effects (like borders). See Figure 6-14.

5. Tap the menu button on the tablet's frame (not the menu icon on the screen). The button is shown to the left.

6. Tap Save to make your changes permanent. If you would rather not save it as is, tap the escape or back button.

You can also send any image by email by attaching it to a message that you are sending. Read how to do that in Chapter 4.

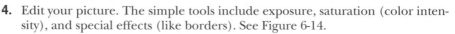

App Store icon

Figure 6-13

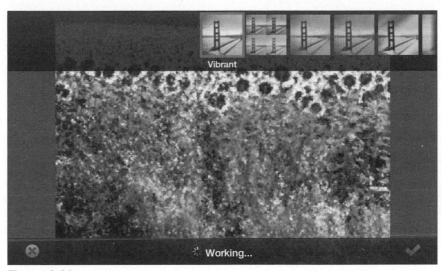

Figure 6-14

Chapter 7

Making and Sharing Videos

Most full-featured tablets can record and play and even edit videos. That means that your children can capture the grandkids singing their latest duet and you can save that moment for posterity. It also means you can record yourself singing some real classics and let your friends and family enjoy that. Go ahead: Embarrass them. Are you ready for your close-up?

Note that entry-level tablets such as the Amazon Kindle Fire and the Barnes & Noble NOOK Tablet do not have cameras; in some parts of life, you only get what you pay for.

tech to connect

activities

- Task 1: Shooting a Video
- Task 2: Changing Video Camera Settings
- Task 3: Adding Special Video Effects
- Task 4: Reviewing a Video Just Taken
- Task 5: Editing Video on a Tablet
- Task 6: Editing Video on a Computer
- Task 7: Sharing Your Video with Other People
- Task 8: Posting a Video on YouTube

Task 1: Shooting a Video

Some tablets have two cameras: One faces the rear (that's your subject, if you're recording) and one faces the front (that's you, if you're facing the screen).

On most tablets, to shoot either a photograph or a video means you have to tap the camera application (on the home screen). However, some tablets have separate camera and video apps.

Here are the basic steps to shoot a video:

1. Go to the home screen and tap the camera icon. Some tablets have the camera icon in a section called Media.
2. Tap the video camera icon.
3. If your tablet has one, tap the icon that switches from rear facing to front facing. If you're shooting a video of what you see in front of you, choose the rear-facing camera. See the icon in Figure 7-1.
4. Get a good grip on the tablet and hold it as steady as possible. Here are ways to make yourself into a human tripod:
   - Move your elbows in as close to your body as you can.
   - Stand with your feet wide apart.
   - Take a deep breath before you begin shooting the video. If you can't hold your breath for the entire shot, breathe slowly.
5. Tap the record button. The button is usually a red circle, like the one in pointed out in Figure 7-2. On most tablets a clock shows the amount of time you have recorded.
6. Tap the stop button. That is usually the same circle that you tapped to begin recording. To pause the recording so that you can start it again, tap the pause button. That button is usually two bars side by side.

If you use the rear-facing video camera, make sure you remove your tablet from the protective case in which you might have put it — that is, unless you want to shoot a video of life inside a padded carrying case.

Tap to switch from rear-facing to front-facing camera

Video camera icon

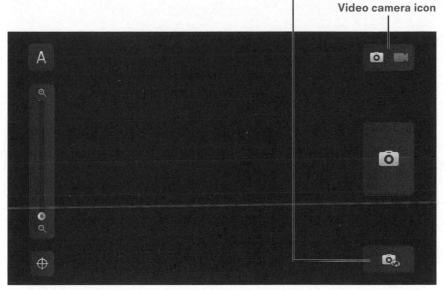

Figure 7-1

Recording/stop recording button

Amount of time you have recorded

Settings icon

Figure 7-2

Task 2: Changing Video Camera Settings

Your video camera has settings that work just fine most of the time, but if your latest recording didn't turn out so well, making some adjustments might help next time. Your tablet may have some or all of the options explained here.

Here's how to change video camera settings:

1. Tap the video camera icon.

2. Find the options. They may be on the screen, you may have to tap a settings icon, you may have to swipe down from the frame (a la Blackberry PlayBook), or you may have to press a menu on the tablet's frame. Figure 7-2 points out a settings icon.

3. Tap a resolution or recording mode. You may see a resolution (like 1020p or 720p), or you might see options (like Fine or Superfine). See Figure 7-3. Some tablets will offer choices like these:

   ■ Normal. The video will look marvelous on a small screen.

   ■ High-definition or HD. It will probably not look different than the normal resolution when you see it on your tablet, but you see a difference if you hook up to a TV.

   ■ Limit for MMS. Multimedia Messaging Service (MMS) files are for sending to smartphones (like an iPhone). These files will look somewhere between barely acceptable and good because they are small and quick to send.

4. Tap an exposure. In theory, your tablet should be able to handle exposure automatically, but the settings here permit a bit of fine-tuning.

5. Tap a white balance option. This helps account for certain kinds of light. Here are some typical options:

   ■ Auto. The tablet will use its best electronic judgment.

   ■ Daylight. This setting works just fine for photos taken outdoors on a sunny day, except for sunrise and sunset.

   ■ Cloudy. Choosing this option should improve the intensity of colors and boost contrast a bit.

   ■ Incandescent. Indoor videos taken in a room lit by old-style light bulbs will have colors that skew toward red or orange.

   ■ Fluorescent. Lighting from fluorescent bulbs is generally skewed toward blue.

6. Tap On for flash or lamp. The flash may help rescue close-ups in a really dark place.

Figure 7-3

Task 3: Adding Special Video Effects

You can add some special effects to videos. The most common set of special effects adjust the color. Those options are often the same as the ones you get for editing photos: normal, negative, black and white, and sepia. See Figure 7-4.

Here are the general steps to turn on color effects when shooting video:

1. Tap the camera icon on the home screen.
2. Tap the video camera icon.
3. Tap the Scene (or Scn or Effects) icon.
4. Tap one of the effects.
5. Tap Save or Apply.
6. Shoot your video, which is explained in this chapter's section titled "Shooting a Video."

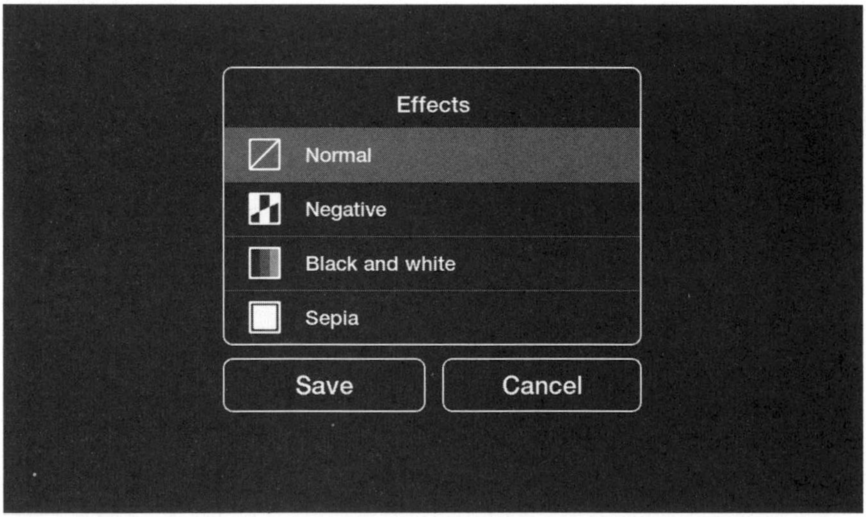

Figure 7-4

Back to normal

Your tablet's video camera keeps the most recent changes you have made to the settings. If you want to return to normal color (or another effect), tap the scene icon, tap your option, and tap Save or Apply.

Task 4: Reviewing a Video Just Taken

You just recorded your sweetheart riding by on her new motorcycle. How did it turn out? Most camera applications let you watch a video from the video screen. Look for and tap a button labeled something like Previous Video; or, you may see a small image (called a thumbnail because it's about that size) of the first frame.

Depending on your tablet, you may be able to see only the most recent video you recorded or you may be able to peek into the entire library of self-made videos and pick any of them for review. See Figure 7-5.

Here's how to take a gander at your cinéma vérité:

1. Tap Previous Video or the thumbnail.
2. Tap Play or the play icon (which is a right-facing arrow).
3. To stop the video, tap Stop or the square.

Thumbnails

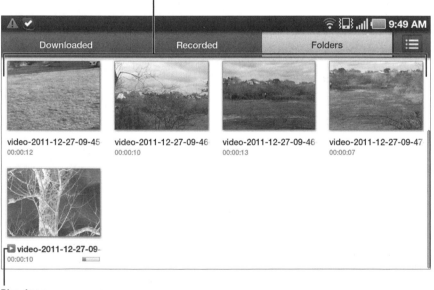

Play icon

Figure 7-5

Task 5: Editing Video on a Tablet

Every work of art can benefit from a good editor — even the sometimes-humble scribbler of this book. (Thank you, Tonya and Katie and the rest of the team.) So too it is with the video you record with your tablet. You captured some great footage, but you probably also managed to record a picture of your thumb . . . and there was that totally uncute moment where one of the kids threw a temper tantrum about mashed parsnips when Mom was carving the turkey.

Editing your videos can mean removing unnecessary parts, switching from one scene to another, and adding scenes from a different video recording.

You can download a basic editing app for most tablets. You will find offerings like iMovie for iPad tablets, Google Movie Studio for Android-based tablets, and Jaycut. See Figure 7-6.

Start point   End point

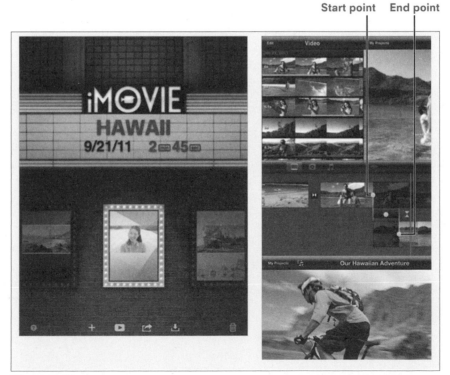

Figure 7-6

Here is how to edit a video clip on an iPad 2. The basic principles apply to other tablets:

1. Tap the camera icon.
2. Tap the camera roll icon. It's in the lower-left corner of the screen.
3. Tap the video you want to edit.
4. On the video's timeline, drag the start point to the beginning part of the video you want to keep.
5. On the same timeline, drag the end point to the last part of the video you want to keep.

6. Tap the play button to watch the part you just chose. You can move the start and end points before you save the edited file; after you save, though, video that was not saved is gone forever. Left on the cutting room floor, in an electronic sort of way.
7. Tap one of the following options:
   - Trim Original. Permanently removes everything that is not inside the points you indicated. Forever.
   - Save as New Clip. Creates a new video recording of only the part you indicated. The original video is not changed. Both videos are saved.
   - Cancel. Did you change your mind? Tap the Cancel button to start over.

Task 6: Editing Video on a Computer

If you want to do some heavy-duty video editing, your tablet may not be the best place. Instead, I recommend a five-step process that is not nearly as complex as it may seem:

1. Shoot your videos. The file will automatically be stored in the tablet's memory.
2. Side load the video from your tablet to a desktop or laptop computer. Read Chapter 3 for those steps.
3. Use a video editor on your computer to edit your video recording.
4. Save the file with an extension that will work on your tablet. The most commonly supported format is MP4; check the specifications for your tablet to see if WMV or 3GP can be used. You can experiment for yourself: Try one of these three formats. If they work, that's fine. If they don't work, try a different one. See Figure 7-7 for my format and its extension.
5. Side load your edited video back to your tablet.

 Full-featured editing programs that run on desktop or laptop computers include Windows Movie Maker (for Windows-based computers) and iMovie (for Macintosh computers).

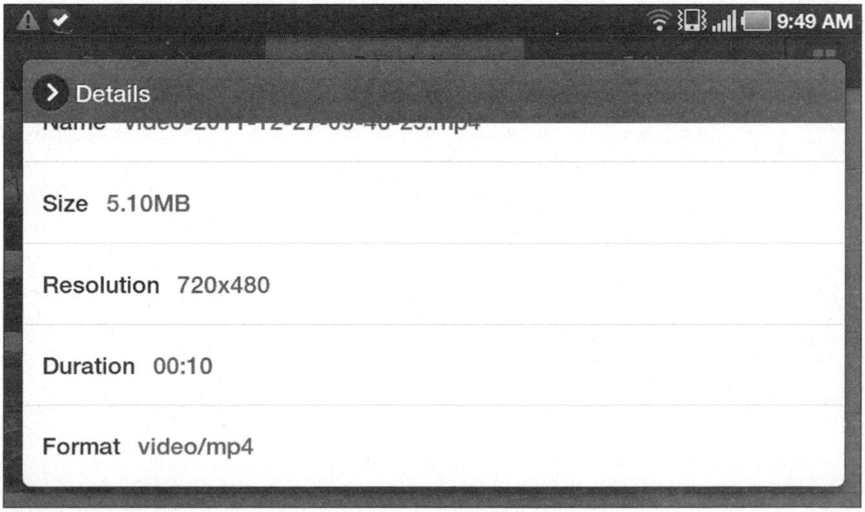

Figure 7-7

Task 7: Sharing Your Video with Other People

Little Steven Spielberg started out making movies just for himself (and for a Boy Scouts merit badge) until eventually someone said, "Why don't you invite some people over and charge admission?" I'm not comparing your Thanksgiving dinner video to "Jaws" (although there is a common theme of uncontrolled hunger). And luckily, you don't need a studio contract to share your work with the world. See Figure 7-8.

Here are some ways to share your videos from within the video app (that is on many tablets):

1. Tap the camera icon on the home screen.
2. Tap Share or another option with a similar name.
3. Tap Send.

Some Android-based devices, including the Samsung Galaxy Tab, let you share your videos this way:

1. Tap the video or the gallery icon.
2. Tap the image of the first scene of your video.
3. Tap the menu button on the tablet's frame (not the menu icon on the screen).
4. Tap Share.
5. Select the video you want to edit.
6. The Share menu options change according to what you have on your tablet. Here are some examples of what you may see: Gmail, Messaging, or YouTube.
7. Tap one of the options.
8. Tap in the To box and type the email address of the person with whom you want to share the video. Chapter 4 explains more about email.

Some email systems don't let you send or get large attachments. Video files can be very large if they are high-definition (HD) and last for very long. That's why you get the option of a lower resolution and length limits.

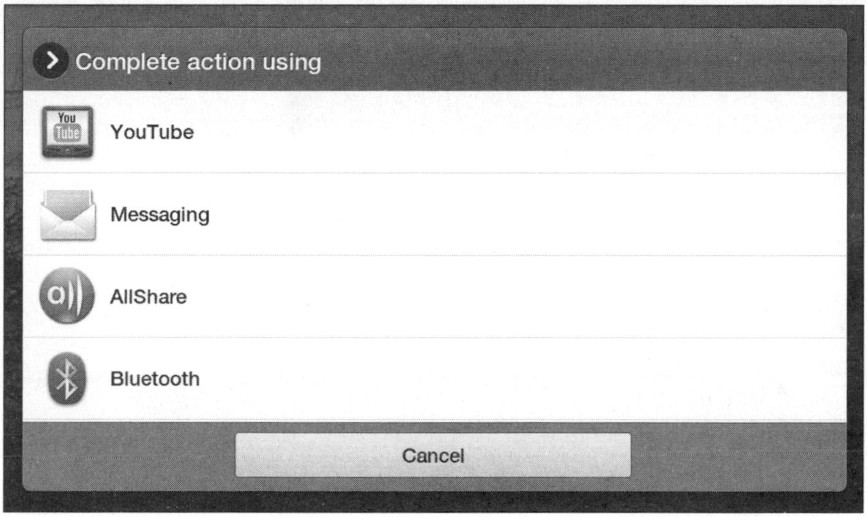

> Complete action using

YouTube

Messaging

AllShare

Bluetooth

Cancel

Figure 7-8

Task 8: Posting a Video on YouTube

You can also share your video recordings on many websites. Several of the sites, including YouTube, are there just to broadcast the photos and videos of anyone and everyone. Figure 7-9 shows the results I got when I searched for kittens in paper shopping bags.

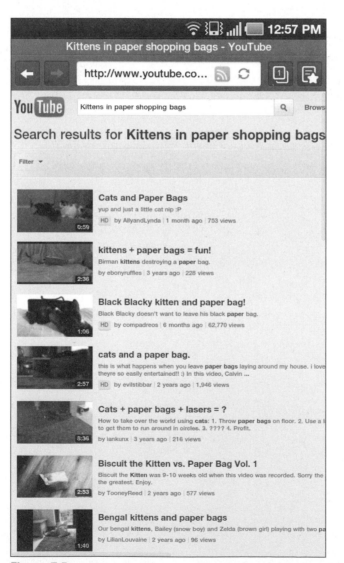

Figure 7-9

Google makes Android and the company owns YouTube. That means if you have an Android-based tablet, you probably already have an account with Google. That also gives you a YouTube account. (You must have an account — sign up — before you can post videos on YouTube.)

Even if you have an Apple iPad, BlackBerry PlayBook, or another kind of non-Android tablet, you can sign up for a free Google account. Here's how:

1. Tap the web browser icon on the home screen.
2. Tap in the address bar and type google.com.
3. Tap Sign In.
4. Tap the Create an Account button.
5. Tap in the User Name box and type the name you want to go by on YouTube.
6. Tap in the Password box and type a safe password. You'll probably have to type it again in another box. Chapter 12 tells how to choose a good password.
7. Tap in the right box and type whatever information you care to share with the masses who use YouTube.

Once you have your account, you can upload a video. This example is based on the Android-based Samsung Galaxy Tab; the steps are similar on other tablets, although you may need to get a YouTube app; see Chapter 12 for instructions. Or, you may need to use your web browser to go to youtube.com.

Here is how upload a video to YouTube from the Galaxy Tab:

1. Make sure your tablet has a WiFi connection to the Internet. Chapter 3 explains how to make sure of that.
2. Tap the gallery app or the video app.
3. Tap the video you want to upload.
4. While the video is on, press the menu button that is on the tablet's frame. The menu button is shown to the left.
5. Tap YouTube.
6. Type a title for the video.
7. Tap the More Details button.
8. Type a description of the video. The more information you type here, the more likely someone will stumble on your video.
9. Tap the Upload button. The longer the recording, the larger the file. The larger the file, the longer it takes for the video to get to YouTube.

Chapter 8

Watching Videos and Movies

What's the difference between your tablet and your TV? Size, mostly. Your tablet can do most anything your TV can (albeit on a small screen with a limited budget). Maybe you're on a cross-country road trip and crave some "I Love Lucy" reruns. You can bring a movie with you on an airplane flight. Or perhaps you'd rather watch the news while your partner views the "World's Strongest Man" on the big screen. Or maybe just the cable is out.

And, of course, there are the videos sent to you by the kids and the grandkids. If you see me in an airport, introduce yourself and you'll be amazed at how easy it is to convince me to show you the latest.

tech to connect

activities

- Task 1: Watching an Online Video
- Task 2: Downloading a Video from the Web
- Task 3: Watching a Video or Movie
- Task 4: Signing Up for a Netflix Account
- Task 5: Watching a Netflix Video
- Task 6: Channel Surfing on Hulu Plus

Task 1: Watching an Online Video

To watch an online movie or other video on your tablet, either you have to transfer (aka download) and save the file, or the movie has to be available in a "stream" sent over the web. Figure 8-1 shows a streaming video.

When you are on the web, you can watch something called streaming video, which is when a website sends a video over the Internet. Your tablet can receive and play the video as it comes in. Think of it as somewhat like broadcast television: The movie, news show, or big game arrives and is immediately shown on the screen. Nothing is saved on your tablet (or telly).

There are two ways to get to streaming video sites like YouTube. You may be able to download and install an app that goes directly to the site. Check your tablet's app store or the website itself. The other way to visit a streaming video site is to start the web browser and type in the address. Usually, you automatically see a small screen version.

In this case I use YouTube as an example. Here's how to watch a video on that website:

1. Tap the Web browser icon.
2. Tap in the address box and type `youtube.com`.
3. Tap any video to watch it immediately. Or, go to the next step to look for specific videos.
4. Tap in the address box and type `google.com`.
5. Type a topic and tap Video to see results that match.
6. Tap a video from YouTube. If your Internet connection is slow, the stream may not display all at once and it may stop.

tech tip There is another way to look for a particular video on YouTube: Go to the website in your web browser. The site has a search bar; type what you're looking for. Scroll to the bottom of the screen and tap Desktop or Full Site. Some tablets let you request the full site, rather than the mobile site, for all the web pages you visit.

Figure 8-1

Task 2: Downloading a Video from the Web

You can download a video from a website, which means save it on your tablet. You can watch a downloaded video anytime. Depending on the site, you may have to buy the video, or you may be able to get it for free. But caution: Free doesn't always mean legal. Check the website's Legal and Terms and Conditions sections first.

You can look for video on these websites:

- iTunes
- Websites that offer free promotional trailers
- Your tablet's online store (Apple iPad, the Android marketplace, and BlackBerry)

If you download a video from your tablet's app store, it will definitely play on your tablet. (You can get to the app store by tapping the icon on your home screen. Read Chapter 12 for how to download an application.) But if you get video from somewhere else, see if you can specify your tablet model.

1. Tap the YouTube icon on your home screen. If there isn't one, tap the Web browser icon, tap in the address box, and type `youtube.com`.
2. Tap in the search box at the top of the page.
3. Type the movie title (or the contents of the kind of video) you want to see.
4. Tap the search icon, which looks like a magnifying glass. Figure 8-2 shows the results of my search for solovetskiy.

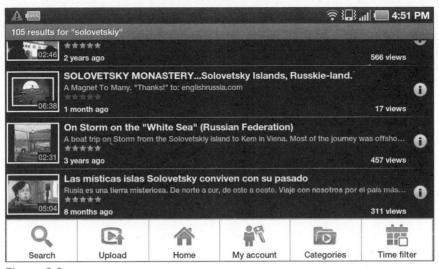

Figure 8-2

Task 3: Watching a Video or Movie

Watching a video or movie on your tablet is a simple tap-dance. These steps assume you have already downloaded any video or movie that you want to see.

1. From the home screen, tap the folder called Video. Some tablets have a folder called Media. On the NOOK Tablet, go to the Library, tap the My Stuff icon, and then tap My Files to find the Videos folder.

2. Tap the video you want to watch. You may need to scroll through a list.

3. Tap the buttons shown in Table 8-1 and Figure 8-3 to control the movie. The buttons are borrowed from the world of the almost-forgotten VCR.

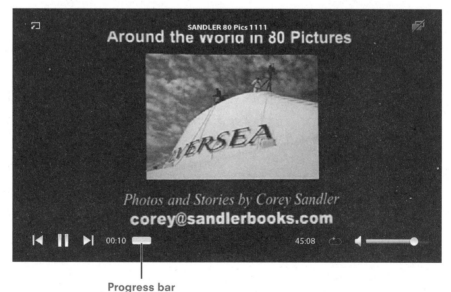

Progress bar

Figure 8-3

Table 8-1

Button to Tap	What the Button Means	Explanation
▶	Play	Tap to begin playing the video, or tap to restart a video that you have paused.
❚❚	Pause	Tap to suspend the video. Most tablets can pause only one video at a time; if you switch to a different video and start playing it, the paused video will stop.
■	Stop	Tap to stop playing a video. Most tablets keep track of where you are and automatically start there next time you tap that video and tap the play button.
▶▶	Fast forward	Move through the video faster. Use fast forward to go to a particular scene. On most tablets, stop fast forwarding by tapping the play button.
▶▶❙	Fast forward to end of file or section	Zoom to the end of a video (or, in certain types of videos, to the end of a section or chapter). Zooming to the end of a video will make it so that the next time you play the video, it will start at the beginning (instead of where it was last stopped).
◀◀	Rewind	Move backward faster. Rewind is useful when you want to replay a scene or section. On most tablets, you stop rewinding by tapping the play button.
❙◀◀	Rewind to beginning of file or section	Return the file to the very start. Some tablets automatically start playing the video again; other tablets make it so that the next time you play the video, it will start at the beginning (instead of where it was last stopped). In this way, rewind to the beginning is the same as fast forward to the end.
▲	Move to a particular point in the file	Most tablets show a progress bar below the screen. Press, hold , and drag the position marker left (to rewind) or right (to fast forward). You'll also see where you are in the movie, usually in minutes and seconds elapsed. Some tablets tell you the percentage of the movie that you have watched.

Task 4: Signing Up for a Netflix Account

Netflix (and some of its competitors, including Apple and Amazon) has a library of movies and shows that you can watch on your tablet (or TV or smartphone). Netflix is covered here because these tablets offer a Netflix app right now: NOOK Tablet, Amazon Kindle Fire, and Apple iPad.

Your Netflix account is portable. You can use the same account on more than one tablet, or on a desktop or laptop computer. The only thing you can't do is use one account on more than one device at the same time.

You must sign up for an account to watch videos from Netflix. Here's how:

1. Some tablets come with a Netflix app on the home screen. Tap it to start signing up. See Figure 8-4. (Just because it's there doesn't mean you're signed up for an account.) If there's no Netflix app icon on your home screen, tap the app store icon and search for it there. Chapter 12 tells you how to download an app.

2. Type in a user name and a password. Chapter 12 tells you how to make up a good password.

3. Type in your credit card number so that card can be billed. If Netflix is offering a free trial period, take advantage of it. You'll get to see how the system works. See Figure 8-5.

Hold that thought

Because the video is streaming, you can start watching on one device (your tablet, for instance) and continue on another (your smartphone, for instance). Just as you cannot be in two places at once, you cannot watch two videos at the same time while using the same account.

There are some limitations, though. I know a certain author who started watching a movie in an airport lounge and then continued watching it on the airplane while we waited for 300 people to squeeze 600 huge carry-on bags into the overhead compartments. Then once we prepared to take off, this same author followed the flight attendant's instructions to turn off electronic devices . . . and then realized that the film would not follow him to Rome — at least not at 40,000 feet. The next time, I downloaded the video. Did I say *I?*

Figure 8-4

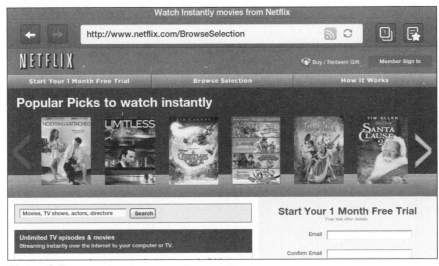

Figure 8-5

Task 5: Watching a Netflix Video

When you get to the Netflix website, you can set up a queue — a list of titles that you can prioritize anytime. Do you want to watch that western now, instead of waiting until after that documentary?

Remember, you have to sign up for a Netflix account before you can watch videos from it. These steps assume you've signed up. If you haven't, follow the steps in the preceding section, "Signing up for a Netflix Account," and then come here. If you want to move a title from one spot in the queue to another, you have to go to the full version of the Netflix site. You do that on your desktop or laptop computer.

Here's how you use Netflix to watch videos:

1. Establish a WiFi connection between your tablet and the Internet. Chapter 3 tells you how to do that. Be aware that if the WiFi signal is weak, the video will pause a lot.
2. Tap the Netflix icon on your tablet. If there isn't one, tap the Web browser icon, tap in the address box, and type `netflix.com`.
3. Tap in the Email Address box and type your address. See Figure 8-6.
4. Tap in the Password box and type your password. If you see it, tap the Remember Me box.
5. Look for movies and TV shows you want to see. Tap Genres or tap Search and type in the box.
6. Tap the play icon next to a title to start the movie. Or, if you want to add it to your queue but not watch it right now, tap the right-facing arrow on the right side of the screen. Then tap Add to Instant.
7. Tap the screen to see the pause and stop icons. Different tablets have different ways to pause or stop. In general, you can stop a movie or close the Netflix app and start the movie in the same place next time.

 Turn your tablet sideways to watch streaming videos from Netflix or Hulu Plus.

Figure 8-6

Task 6: Channel Surfing on Hulu Plus

Hulu is a television network that offers entertainment from its three main owners: NBC, ABC, and Fox. Hulu (that's hoo-loo) also provides programming from CBS and many cable TV channels. You can get Hulu free on your desktop and laptop computer. However, tablet users have to subscribe to Hulu Plus and pay a monthly fee. See Figure 8-7.

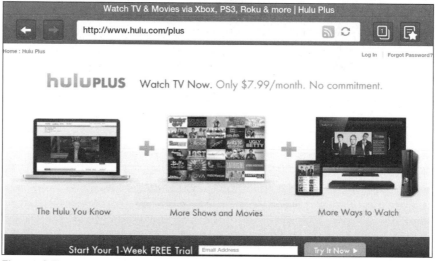

Figure 8-7

Hulu Plus has full seasons of many hit shows, plus classic TV series and movies — some classic, some current. And like Netflix, your WiFi signal strength helps determine how smooth the stream is. See Figure 8-8. Also like Netflix, you can get to your Hulu Plus account and watch a show on your tablet, on a desktop or laptop computer, or on a television that connects to the Internet.

Setting up and using a Hulu Plus account and subscription is nearly the same as for Netflix. You need separate accounts for each service if you want to use both.

WiFi signal strength is good

Figure 8-8

If your tablet shows fewer than three bars of WiFi signal strength, make sure there are no major physical barriers (like an appliance) between the router and your tablet. Or, you can buy a better WiFi router; the latest and mostly greatest technology are WiFi N routers, which are faster and offer greater range than A, B, or G versions. If necessary, you can buy and install a WiFi extender, which rebroadcasts the signal further into the recesses of your home or office.

These steps assume you have signed up for an account. If you haven't, go to the section in this chapter called "Signing Up for a Netflix Account." Follow those same basic steps at the hulu.com website. While you're there, tap the Learn More button to go to the registration page. Register and then come back here.

Here's how to watch Hulu Plus on your tablet:

1. Establish a WiFi connection between your tablet and the Internet. Chapter 3 tells you how to do that. Be aware that if the WiFi signal is weak, the video will pause a lot.
2. Tap the Hulu Plus icon on your home screen. If there isn't one, tap the Web browser icon, tap in the address box, and type hulu.com.
3. Tap in the Email box and type your email address.
4. Tap in the Password box and type your password. You can't get to the Hulu Plus features if you're signed in to a free Hulu account.
5. Look for movies and TV shows you want to see. Tap a title to add it to your queue.
6. Tap the photo next to a title to start the show.
7. Tap the screen to see the pause and stop icons. Different tablets have different ways to pause or stop. In general, you can stop a movie or close the Hulu app and start the movie in the same place next time.

Chapter 9

Buying and Playing Music and Podcasts

For many of us, our first inkling of moveable music was the Sony Walkman, which arrived in 1979. We'd already seen the portable calculator and the steadily shrinking battery-powered radio, but the Walkman — a music cassette player clipped to your belt — seemed a different class of device. How so? Because you could personalize the soundtrack of your life by making (or buying) just the music you wanted to hear.

A tablet can store a huge amount of music, show you liner notes (even without an album), and produce better sound than a smaller music player (like an iPod).

tech to connect

activities

- Task 1: Playing Music from a Tablet
- Task 2: Moving Music from a Computer
- Task 3: Buying Music on the Web
- Task 4: Finding Music in the Clouds
- Task 5: Playing Music from the Clouds
- Task 6: Downloading Cloud Music
- Task 7: Listening to Internet Radio
- Task 8: Creating Your Own Radio Station
- Task 9: Tuning in to Podcasts

Task 1: Playing Music from a Tablet

Any member of AARP or anyone anywhere near the age of eligibility for the association grew up with record albums: stacks of wax, Golden Oldies. You put them on a record player and watched them revolve below the needle that read the wobbles in the tracks and converted them to music. Today, you can listen to those same songs — and tens of thousands that have been recorded since — without the record (or the 8-track, cassette tape, CD, or DVD).

These steps assume you already have music on your tablet. If you bought the music from a record company or an online website, you will probably see the song's full name, artist, album, and length while it plays. Some tablets have links that you can tap to buy other music by the same artist.

Here's how to play music that has been loaded into the memory of your tablet or delivered from the cloud:

1. Tap the music app. See Figure 9-1.
2. Scroll through songs or tap one of the options to see the music organized this way:
   - Artist
   - Album
   - Playlist (a mix-tape sort of group that you make)
3. Tap a song to listen to it. Tap a playlist to hear the whole group. Most music players have VCR-like controls that you can tap to play, pause, restart, or jump to the next song. Tap the looping arrows to repeat the current song or album; tap them again to stop the repeat. Tap the interwoven arrows to shuffle the deck and play songs from the list in random order. See Figure 9-2.
4. What's that? You can't hear it? Some tablets have volume control on their screen; touch the screen to show the controls. Other tablets have physical buttons along the side that you must push.

Getting picky

One good thing about music as individual files: No duds. No more buying albums that consisted of a dozen cuts, of which perhaps one or two were real gems, three or four were worth listening to, and the remainder were just filling space on the acetate disk. Today you can buy an entire album or just individual songs. And no unwanted interruptions. When you make your own collection of music, there are no disk jockeys and no commercials. And finally, no deterioration. I'll bet all of us at one time scratched a favorite record album (or left it in the car to get warped beyond playing). Cassette tapes wore out. CDs got cracked. Electronic files, on the other hand, don't wear out. If only we could say the same about our own mortal bodies.

Music app icon

Figure 9-1

Tap to
shuffle songs

Tap to repeat a
song or album

Figure 9-2

Hi-Fi via WiFi

The sound is pretty good when you consider your tablet's tiny speakers. But you can improve things: Plug a set of headphones (or newfangled earbuds, like you can see in Figure 9-3) into the jack on the side of the tablet. Or, connect your tablet by wire from that same jack to your home's stereo system or TV.

Put in your ears

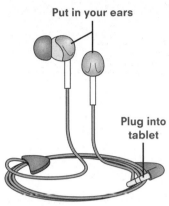

Plug into
tablet

Figure 9-3

Task 2: Moving Music from a Computer

You probably already have a music collection. Maybe you put your music on your personal computer (or at least in boxes filled with CDs). If your music is the kind of file your tablet works with, you can usually move the tracks or side load them from the computer to your tablet. You'll use the USB cable that came with your tablet. Be sure to follow the rules in the Safety, Regulatory, and Legal guide that came along with your tablet to avoid copyright infringement issues.

Here's how:

1. Find the music files on your computer. They may be in a folder called My Music or something equally obvious.
2. Turn on your tablet and wait for it to fully load.
3. Plug the smaller end of the USB cable to your tablet. Never try to force a cable into an opening; it fits only one way. Usually, the tablet end of the USB cable is the one indicated in Figure 9-4.
4. Plug the larger end of the USB cable to the matching jack (aka port) on your laptop or desktop computer. Your tablet and computer should make nice and appear ready to work with you.
5. Drag and drop the files from the computer to the tablet's Music folder. (You can go from tablet to computer if you want to make backup copies.)

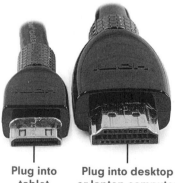

Plug into tablet   **Plug into desktop or laptop computer**

Figure 9-4

If you can't make a copy, try getting in touch with the company that sold you the music to see if unrestricted versions are available. Oh, and don't copy and give away music to everyone you know. That's illegal. So is downloading from certain sites (like those that don't have you pay for music). Just buy from reputable sources and use the music on your own tablet.

Music file formats

If you buy and download music directly from the "official" supplier of music for your tablet, your tablet will be able to play that file. If you run into trouble, contact the seller. On the other hand, *before* you download music from another music seller (like the Amazon MP3 store, for instance), read the description of the service to make sure your tablet will work with the file format. As the Amazon store name suggests, its files are in the MP3 format, which should work just fine.

Task 3: Buying Music on the Web

Most tablets have their own, official store where you can buy entire albums or individual tracks.

These steps assume you have already signed up for an account with the store. If not, create an account and protect it with a strong password. (See Chapter 12 for how to pick a strong password.) When you're signing up, you are likely to be offered this choice: Store your credit card number in your account or enter it each time you buy something. I suggest entering it each time. That is safer.

To buy music and download it directly to your tablet, do this:

1. Tap the music store app of your tablet. And you can also add an app or go directly to an online music store using the web browser of your tablet.
   - Apple iPad comes with Apple iTunes.
   - BlackBerry PlayBook offers 7Digital. See Figure 9-5.
   - Android-based tablets offer 7Digital or Amazon MP3.
2. Sign in to your personal account. That usually entails tapping in the boxes and entering your email address and password.
3. Find what you want to buy. You can enter an artist, composer, song title, or album title. Most stores also let you browse through genres: classical, folk, rock and roll, country, and many others. Sometimes you get to hear a snippet of songs for free.
4. Tap the Buy or Purchase button. After you pay, the file is sent to your tablet (with no help on your part). A song may arrive within a minute or so. You can get to the song by going to the music app on the home screen.

Amazin'

You can get a free Amazon MP3 app for Android tablets. Tap the Android store icon on your tablet's home screen. No matter what kind of tablet you have, you can buy music from the Amazon MP3 store. Tap your Web browser icon, tap in the address box, and type `amazon.com`. Then tap the Amazon MP3 store. See Figure 9-6.

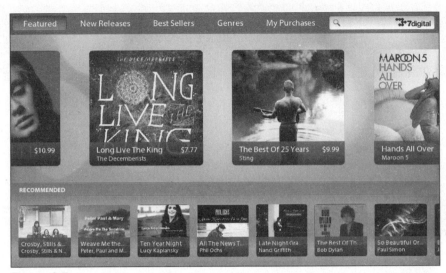

Figure 9-5

Figure 9-6

Task 4: Finding Music in the Clouds

The term *cloud* is the latest way to talk about cyberspace. Basically, the cloud stores information (music in this case) instead of your tablet having to hold it in its memory. When you want to play your music, you ask for it to be delivered from out there. Somewhere. Among the cloud(s).

Your music is available to you anytime you have a wireless connection to the Internet. And it works in both directions: You can store in the cloud any music you have bought and download it to your device. Or, you can upload music you already own to the cloud so you can get ahold of it from any of your devices (tablet, smartphone, laptop computer, and more).

This example assumes you have signed up an account with a major music provider, such as iTunes, Amazon MP3, or 7Digital. (If you sign up with any or all of them, you might get free music or discounts, and you will see an explanation of how to get on their cloud.) This example uses the Amazon Cloud Player. The other services work much the same way. Also, before you get started: Consider using your desktop or laptop computer (instead of your tablet) when you initially sign up. You may have some music stored there, and your computer probably has a faster Internet connection.

Here's how to upload music to the nebulous cloud:

1. Log into your personal account by typing your user name and password.
2. Click Upload Files. The system looks for music that will work on your tablet. See Figure 9-7.

Music that you buy does not automatically go to your cloud account. You can easily solve this problem: Resave the music to your tablet or to a computer associated with the cloud account. Then upload them back to the cloud drive.

555-cyber

Where exactly is cyberspace? Here's my preferred definition: If you made a phone call to me, where would that conversation take place? It's not in my office, and it's not in your den. Our words meet and then pass by each other in some unidentified momentary location along a wire or in a radio wave bouncing off a satellite: That's cyberspace.

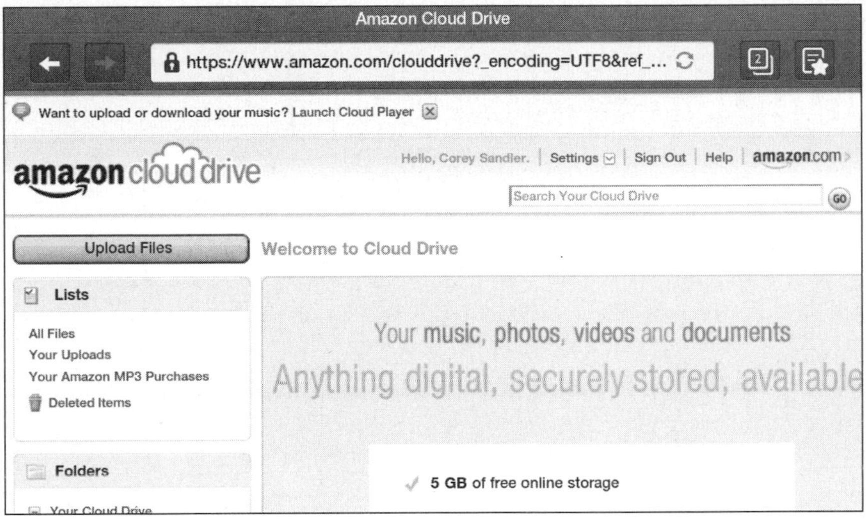
Amazon Cloud Drive
https://www.amazon.com/clouddrive?_encoding=UTF8&ref_...
Want to upload or download your music? Launch Cloud Player
amazon cloud drive
Hello, Corey Sandler. | Settings | Sign Out | Help | amazon.com
Search Your Cloud Drive
GO
Upload Files
Welcome to Cloud Drive
Lists
All Files
Your Uploads
Your Amazon MP3 Purchases
Deleted Items
Folders
Your music, photos, videos and documents
Anything digital, securely stored, available
5 GB of free online storage

Figure 9-7

Task 5: Playing Music from the Clouds

After you sign up for and put music in your cloud account, you can use the cloud music player to play your music. Here's how:

1. Tap the Web browser icon on your tablet's home screen.
2. Tap the app for the cloud player. Or, use the web browser to go to the site that belongs to the cloud provider.
3. Sign in to your cloud account.
4. Tap the Cloud Drive Music or On-Device Music button.
5. Tap Songs. Or, tap one of these buttons:
   - Playlists (You can make one within the app.)
   - Artists
   - Albums
6. Tap any song title to begin playing. You will have VCR-like controls to play, pause, replay, or move to the next track. See Figure 9-8.

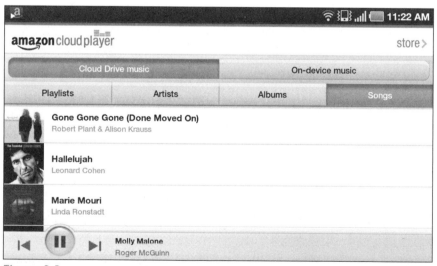

Figure 9-8

 A cellular data connection is usually slower and much more expensive than a WiFi link. However, if you plan to use your tablet while traveling in a place without WiFi, a cellular link may be your only option for reaching the cloud. Keep in mind that you can play any music that is actually stored on your tablet. Or you can sing.

Task 6: Downloading Cloud Music

When you own a track of music, you can play it whenever and wherever you want. In the old days, that meant you could take a vinyl disc (they were called records) from your bedroom to the living room, to a friend's house for a party, or to the gymnasium for a sock hop. In modern times, it means that you can transfer that track from your computer to your tablet to your smartphone.

You can't legally make copies for all of your friends, or for all of the people in your town, or for anyone on the Internet.

First, check the rules of your cloud service to make sure you don't run afoul of any copyright laws. Then go ahead and download music from cloud storage to your tablet:

1. Make a connection to the Internet by WiFi (or cellular data link if available and needed).
2. Tap the app for the cloud service. Or, tap the Web browser icon on your tablet's home screen, tap in the address box, and type the company's web address.
3. Tap the Playlist, Artists, or Albums button.
4. Tap the Download button. The Amazon Cloud Player has a green downward-facing arrow in the upper-right corner of each album, artist, or playlist page. You can see the arrow in Figure 9-9. You can also press and hold any song, album, artist, or playlist and tap Download Song. See Figure 9-10.

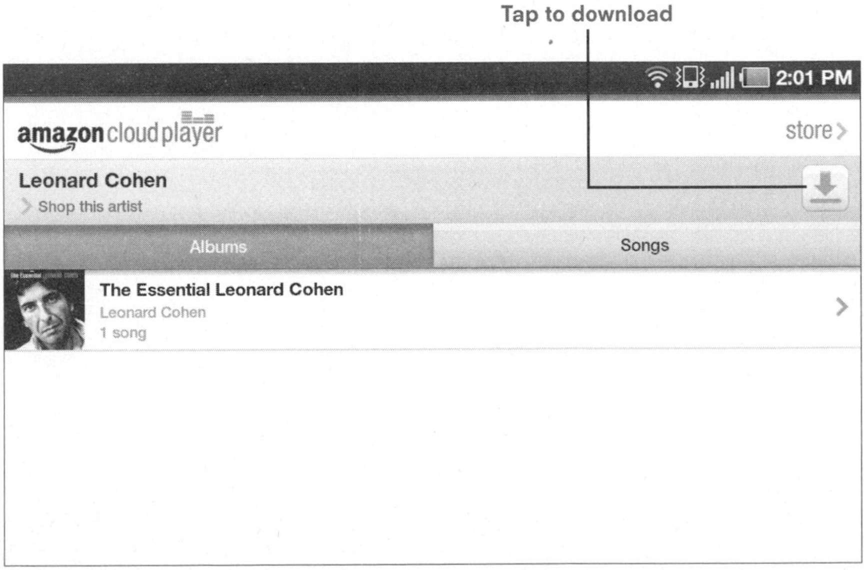

Tap to download

Figure 9-9

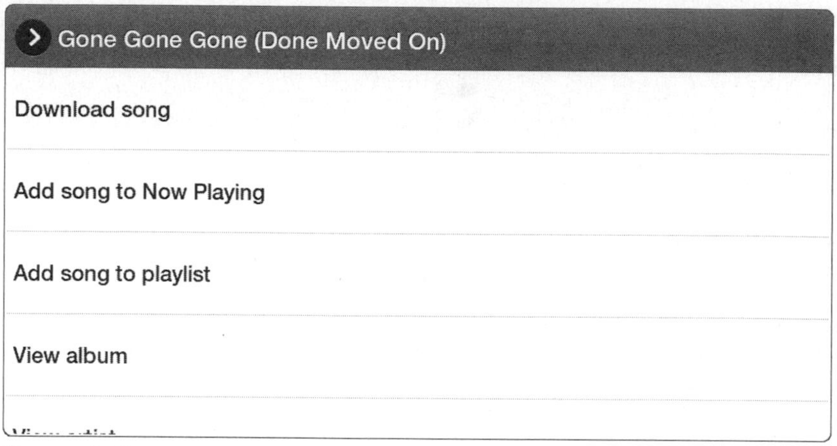

> Gone Gone Gone (Done Moved On)

Download song

Add song to Now Playing

Add song to playlist

View album

Figure 9-10

Task 7: Listening to Internet Radio

How's this for going full circle? You can listen to radio stations on your tablet. There are major music, talk, sports, and religious stations, as well as Internet-only productions that may be aimed at a very, very narrow body of listeners: left-handed Southerners of Icelandic origin who are considering vegetarianism, perhaps. Even AARP has its own radio station. Most stations let you search by genre, to choose among top stations, or to assign stations to your own personal favorites list. See Figure 9-11 for my folk station options.

You don't have to install a huge shortwave antenna up on the roof. You just need two things: a WiFi or cellular connection to the Internet and an app that tunes your tablet into the station.

 If you use a cellular Internet connection instead of WiFi, you could get a big bill from your service provider. Make sure you understand the roaming policies if you plan on using a cellular connection. WiFi users can usually get free or low-cost access to the web.

Radio apps

You can download a radio app from your tablet's app store. Tap the app store icon on your home screen. Radio applications include Winamp, AOL Radio, live365, and Shoutcast. There are so many of them that I'm sure three new ones were created during the time it took me to write this chapter.

Figure 9-11

Here's how to use Winamp:

1. Tap the Web browser icon on the tablet's home screen.
2. Tap in the address box and type `winamp.com`. Or, type `google.com` and then type internet radio. See what results you get. Some you can simply listen to, and some make you sign up as a member before you can listen.
3. Tap a feed to listen to it. See Figure 9-12.

Figure 9-12

Task 8: Creating Your Own Radio Station

You don't have to listen to someone else's music decisions. You can build your own radio station. Just start with a song or artist and, using the power of a computer, find similar songs and related singers. I don't know exactly what to call these services: I think of them as computer-assisted personal jukeboxes. There are a number worth considering, but two two popular choices are Pandora and Slacker.

Nearly all radio stations let you set up your account on one device (such as your tablet) and use it on another (such as your regular old music player). Also, it may be easier to set up your radio station account on a desktop or laptop computer. All of the stations and preferences you enter there will appear on your tablet when you sign in using the same user name and the proper password.

Here's how to use a computer-assisted personal jukebox:

1. Make sure you have a wireless link to the Internet. WiFi is usually free or cheap. A cellular Internet connection can be expensive, especially if you are roaming away from home. Read more in Chapter 3 about the Internet links.

2. Tap the radio station icon on your tablet's home screen. If there isn't one, tap the app store icon and download one. The apps are free. Chapter 12 tells you how to do that. Figure 9-13 shows the Pandora icon.

3. Sign up for an account with a user name and password. Nearly all of radio services (including Pandora and Slacker) offer free music.

4. Start customizing a station. On Pandora, type a song title or artist you really enjoy. Slacker has genre stations that you may use as a starting point. Tapping to vote on songs helps the station play songs even more to your liking.

5. Listen to the song or tap the fast forward icon to skip over it. You can skip just a few songs every time you listen, so skip wisely. You can pause a song, but you can't rewind or replay a song. If the song is available to buy, you'll see a picture of the album or CD cover. Tap Buy to pay for and download a copy of the song to your tablet. See Figure 9-14.

Figure 9-13

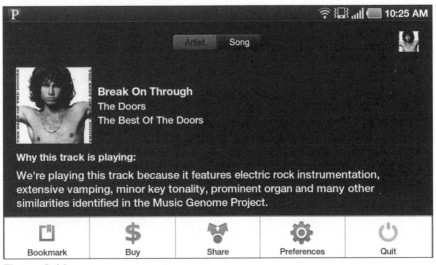

Figure 9-14

The magic behind Pandora

These personal jukeboxes start with a few songs or artists you like and then search out and find music that is similar or shares certain attributes. I've always enjoyed "Season of the Witch," one of the high points of hippie music, written in 1966 by the Scottish singer-songwriter Donovan. I like his version, and also most of the cover versions including Julie Driscoll and Brian Auger; the super-group of Mike Bloomfield, Al Kooper, and Steven Stills; and the New Orleans original Dr. John.

Until I set up and began using my Pandora account I never realized the link between that song and some of my other favorites. The singer-songwriter J.J. Cale was influenced by Donovan, and went on to write songs including "After Midnight," which was made famous by Eric Clapton. Others in the same orbit: Leon Russell and Delaney & Bonnie. And following another thread, psychedelic Donovan vibrated in harmony with Jefferson Airplane, The Zombies, and other groups that made up the soundtrack of my youth. Pandora made the connection.

Task 9: Tuning in to Podcasts

Podcast is a word that snuck into the dictionary about ten years ago. A podcast is any audio package delivered to a tablet (or portable music player or computer or smartphone). You can find podcasts of radio shows, words of wisdom by celebrities or commentators, and spoken versions of another relatively new kind of website, the blog (shorthand for web log).

You can go directly to a website and see if it offers podcasts; just look for an RSS icon like the one in Figure 9-15. Or, you can download a podcast app. Nearly all such apps are free. Chapter 12 explains how to download apps. You might want to try several to find the one that has the best selection for your interests and that is easiest for you to use. Most podcasts are free, but some require payment. If you get a request for a credit card or other payment, you'll know it isn't gratis.

RSS feed icon

Figure 9-15

Here's how to listen to podcasts on your tablet:

1. When you're on a web page whose podcasts you might like, tap the RSS icon. The icon might be an orange set of waves to the right of the web address at the top of the page, or you may find the same icon on the page itself.

2. Tap Stream or Download. See Figure 9-16. Streaming lets you listen immediately. Downloading saves the podcast on your tablet so you can listen to it later. Check the podcast website for its rules about downloading content.

Figure 9-16

Chapter 10

Reading eBooks

You can carry dozens — even thousands — of electronic books (eBooks in common parlance) on your tablet. Although many people (including me from time to time) lament the absence of a beautifully designed, printed, and bound book, here is the most important truth about using your tablet as a portable library: You're still reading. In the end, it's about the thoughts, research, and creativity of the author and the magical link that is created when a reader becomes absorbed in the words.

Amazon offers a Kindle reading app that runs on different tablets, including the Apple iPad, Android-based tablets including the Samsung Galaxy Tab, and the BlackBerry PlayBook. Kobo offers a similar reading app that is available on many tablets, including the BlackBerry PlayBook. Read Chapter 12 for instructions for downloading an app.

Read Chapter 11 for how to find, buy, and download eBooks.

tech to connect

activities

- Task 1: Opening an eBook
- Task 2: Turning the Pages
- Task 3: Using the Table of Contents
- Task 4: Searching within an eBook
- Task 5: Searching Outside an eBook
- Task 6: Changing Text Size and Style
- Task 7: Adding Bookmarks, Highlights, or Notes
- Task 8: Finding a Bookmark or Note

Task 1: Opening an eBook

Let's get right down to the joy of reading. Depending on the eBook, you may see the cover, followed by the title page, complete with the author's name and information about the publisher. Figure 10-1 shows the beginning of a chapter.

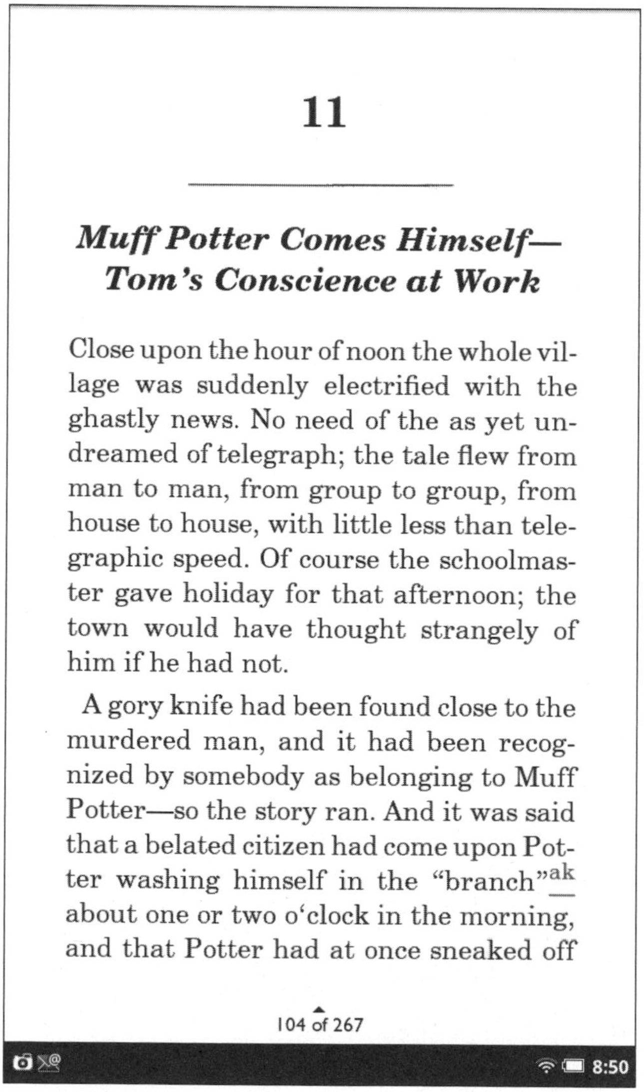

11

Muff Potter Comes Himself— Tom's Conscience at Work

Close upon the hour of noon the whole village was suddenly electrified with the ghastly news. No need of the as yet undreamed of telegraph; the tale flew from man to man, from group to group, from house to house, with little less than telegraphic speed. Of course the schoolmaster gave holiday for that afternoon; the town would have thought strangely of him if he had not.

A gory knife had been found close to the murdered man, and it had been recognized by somebody as belonging to Muff Potter—so the story ran. And it was said that a belated citizen had come upon Potter washing himself in the "branch"[ak] about one or two o'clock in the morning, and that Potter had at once sneaked off

104 of 267

Figure 10-1

And, in general, all tablet computers work generally in the same way: you'll see a page (or in some views, a two-page spread) and you tap or swipe your way to go forward or backward.

Here's how to read a book that's already loaded onto your tablet:

1. Find the book.
    - You may have an app from a bookseller (Amazon Kindle, Barnes & Noble NOOK, Kobo, or other brand name source). Tap that app's icon.
    - Your tablet may instead have a Library or Book folder. Tap the folder name.
    - You may have loaded eBooks from your desktop or laptop computer. Tap the folder called Documents or Downloads or something similar.
2. Tap the book cover or title. See Figure 10-2.
3. Start reading.
4. When you're ready to turn the page, go to the next section of this chapter: "Turning the Pages."

Most tablets can tell which way you are holding them. If you rotate the tablet, the text orientation changes. If you don't want the text to change orientation, read the instruction manual. It will tell you where to find the screen rotation lock button or menu option.

Figure 10-2

Task 2: Turning the Pages

Tablet computers let your fingers do the walking through the pages. There are slight variations between the various designs but the basic gestures are applied: tapping, swiping, flicking, dragging, and on some tablets pushing a soft button on the frame. Chapter 1 of this book tells you how to master those gestures. See Figure 10-3.

To turn the page forward on an Apple iPad, do one of these things from the right side of the margin or screen:

- Tap or flick your finger near the right margin of the screen. This is interpreted as a "hurry up" command; the page turns almost instantly.
- Drag your finger near the margin. The result is a slower, more mannerly turn: The page folds down as if you were turning pages in a real book.
- Drag down from the upper-right corner of the book. Again, a slow turn, with the page curling over from the very spot where you started dragging.
- Drag from the middle-right margin. The entire page will curl away into the next.
- Drag up from the lower-right corner. You'll go to the next page, but it will seem to drag up from the spot you used as a starting place.

To turn the page forward in the Kindle app or Kobo app, do one of these things:

- Tap the right side of the screen.
- Swipe from right to left.

To turn back a page on an Apple iPad, do one of these things from the left side or margin of the screen:

- Tap or flick your finger near the right margin of the screen. This is interpreted as a "hurry up" command; the page turns almost instantly.
- Drag your finger near the margin. The result is a slower, more mannerly turn: The page folds down as if you were turning pages in a real book.
- Drag down from the upper-right corner of the book. Again, a slow turn, with the page curling over from the very spot where you started dragging.
- Drag from the middle-right margin. The entire page will curl away into the next.
- Drag up from the lower-right corner. You'll go to the next page, but it will seem to drag up from the spot you used as a starting place.

Swiping to scroll left and right.
Figure 10-3

To turn back a page in the Kindle app or Kobo app, do one of these things:

- Tap the left side of the screen.
- Swipe from left to right.

Southpaws

On some tablet operating systems, you can change settings so that tapping the left side of a page turns the page. From within the reading application, open the Settings panel or the menu and look for a customization option.

To jump to a specific page on an Apple iPad, or in either the Kindle or Kobo app, do these things:

1. Tap anywhere near the center of the currently displayed page. You will see the page navigator controls.
2. Drag your finger along the slider at the bottom of the screen. You can see the slider in Figure 10-4. The chapter and page numbers change as you move to the right or left.
3. Let go of the slider when you get where you want to go.

Drag the slider to quickly change pages.

Figure 10-4

To jump to a specific page on a Samsung Galaxy Tab, follow these steps:

1. Tap the menu button on the frame of the tablet (not the menu icon on the screen). The menu button looks like the icon you see to the left.
2. Tap the Go To button.
3. Tap the Location button.
4. Type a page number.
5. Tap OK.

Task 3: Using the Table of Contents

A table of contents is a wonderful tool — a way to jump to the section you need right now. As much as I love readers who begin my works by opening page 1 and enjoying my thrilling, elucidating, and entertaining prose all the way to the end, I also realize that many readers of how-to books tend to dive right in to the problem at hand. So, this book is designed to make the contents searchable so readers can deal with immediate questions.

Most eBooks have a table of contents that you can tap. See Figure 10-5. Here's how to jump to a chapter using the table of contents:

1. Open a book to any page.
2. Follow the rest of the steps according to the kind of tablet you have.

If you have an **Apple iPad**, follow these steps:

3. Tap the Table of Contents/Bookmark button near the top of the screen.
4. Tap the chapter you want to read.

If you have a **Kobo app** on the **BlackBerry PlayBook**, follow these steps:

3. Swipe down from the top frame of the tablet.
4. Tap the Contents button.
5. Tap a chapter title or number or any other listing on the page. You may also see Next Chapter or Previous Chapter buttons that you can tap.

If you have a **Samsung Galaxy Tab**, follow these steps:

3. Tap the menu button on the frame of the tablet (not the menu icon on the screen.) The menu button is shown to the left.
4. Tap the Go To button shown in Figure 10-6.
5. Tap the Table of Contents button.
6. Tap the chapter you want to read.

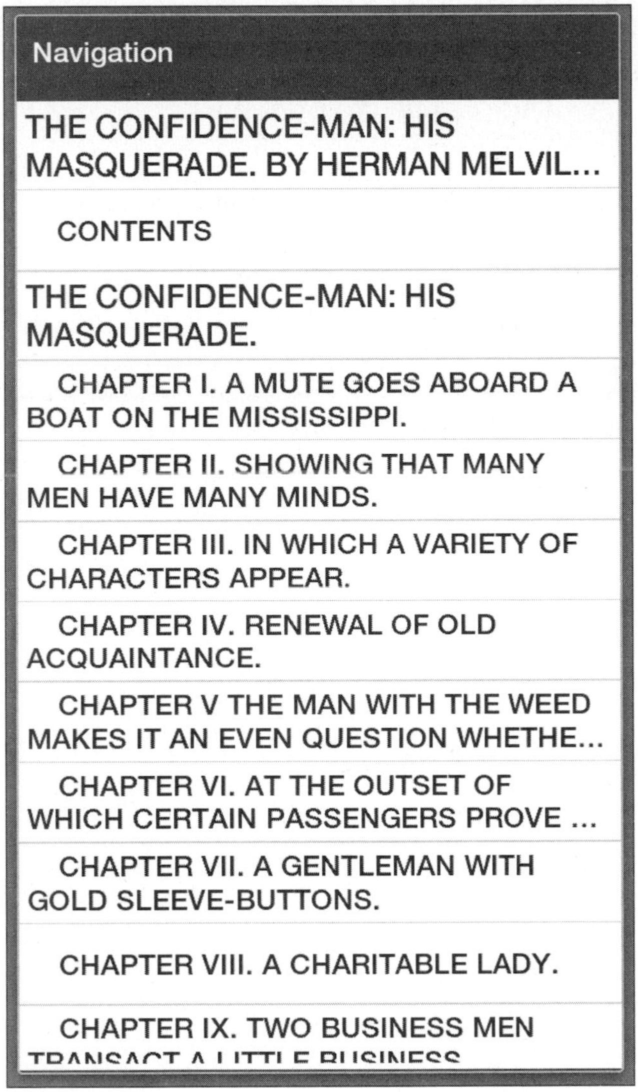

Navigation

THE CONFIDENCE-MAN: HIS
MASQUERADE. BY HERMAN MELVIL...

CONTENTS

THE CONFIDENCE-MAN: HIS
MASQUERADE.

CHAPTER I. A MUTE GOES ABOARD A
BOAT ON THE MISSISSIPPI.

CHAPTER II. SHOWING THAT MANY
MEN HAVE MANY MINDS.

CHAPTER III. IN WHICH A VARIETY OF
CHARACTERS APPEAR.

CHAPTER IV. RENEWAL OF OLD
ACQUAINTANCE.

CHAPTER V THE MAN WITH THE WEED
MAKES IT AN EVEN QUESTION WHETHE...

CHAPTER VI. AT THE OUTSET OF
WHICH CERTAIN PASSENGERS PROVE ...

CHAPTER VII. A GENTLEMAN WITH
GOLD SLEEVE-BUTTONS.

CHAPTER VIII. A CHARITABLE LADY.

CHAPTER IX. TWO BUSINESS MEN
TRANSACT A LITTLE BUSINESS

Figure 10-5

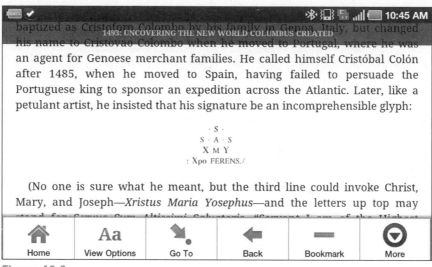

Figure 10-6

Task 4: Searching within an eBook

tech tip

If someone refers to a particular passage, your page numbering probably won't correspond. That's where the search function can help you find the reference you need to keep up with your book club. Some eBooks are just pictures of book pages, instead of searchable text. You can look at the pictures and read the words, but they can't be searched and they can't be changed (to show bigger type, for example). However, in most eBooks you can search for a particular word, phrase, or name: Anything or everything can be hunted. See Figure 10-7.

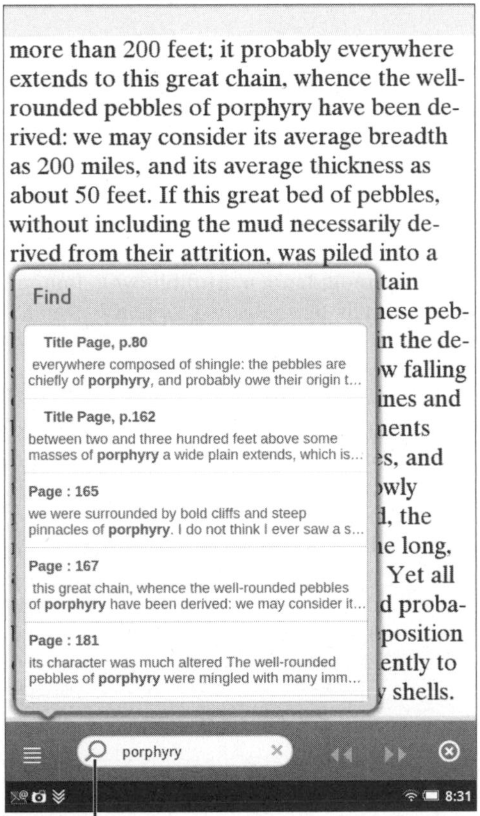

more than 200 feet; it probably everywhere extends to this great chain, whence the well-rounded pebbles of porphyry have been derived: we may consider its average breadth as 200 miles, and its average thickness as about 50 feet. If this great bed of pebbles, without including the mud necessarily derived from their attrition, was piled into a

Find

> **Title Page, p.80**
> everywhere composed of shingle: the pebbles are chiefly of **porphyry**, and probably owe their origin t...

> **Title Page, p.162**
> between two and three hundred feet above some masses of **porphyry** a wide plain extends, which is...

> **Page : 165**
> we were surrounded by bold cliffs and steep pinnacles of **porphyry**. I do not think I ever saw a s...

> **Page : 167**
> this great chain, whence the well-rounded pebbles of **porphyry** have been derived: we may consider it...

> **Page : 181**
> its character was much altered The well-rounded pebbles of **porphyry** were mingled with many imm...

≡   ⌕ porphyry   ✕   ◀◀ ▶▶   ⊗

✆◎⌄   🛜 ▭ 8:31

Tap the search icon.

Figure 10-7

Here's how to search within a book for a word, name, or phrase:

1. Open a book on the screen.
2. Follow the rest of the steps according to the kind of tablet you have.

If you have an **Apple iPad** or a **Kindle app**, follow these steps:

3. Tap the search icon (a magnifying glass).
4. Type the word, phrase, or name you want to find.

If you have a **Samsung Galaxy Tab**, follow these steps:

3. Tap the search icon (a magnifying glass) on the tablet's frame. Don't tap the search icon that is on the screen.
4. Type the word or phrase you want to find.
5. Tap Go.

Task 5: Searching Outside an eBook

Here's another trick you can't easily do with a printed book, at least if that's the only thing (along with a strong WiFi or cellular signal) you've got with you on your desert island. If you want to learn more about the subject, or if you want to fact-check something, you can go out on the web and do your own research. I was looking for the definition of a battologist in Figure 10-8.

words. Word origins not only shed light on their current meaning, but offer clues to their ...

Obsolete Word of the Day: battologist
obsoleteword.blogspot.com/2007/08/**battologist**.html

Aug 28, 2007 – **battologist**. This is someone who repeats the same thing for no reason. It comes from the Greek word for stammerer. posted by the scribbler ...

Battologist - definition of **Battologist** by the Free Online Dictionary ...
www.thefreedictionary.com/**Battologist**

Legal dictionary. Financial dictionary. Acronyms. Idioms. Encyclopedia. Wikipedia encyclopedia ? **Battologist**. 0.01 sec. Bat`tol´o`gist. n. 1. One who battologizes. ...

battologist - Encyclopedia
www.encyclo.co.uk/define/**battologist**

battologist - Meaning and definition. ... Look up: **battologist**. **Battologist** Bat·tol'o· gist noun One who battologizes. Found on http:// www.encyclo.co.uk/webster/B/23 ...

Battologist...Are You One? | | CF Web ProfessionalsCF Web Professionals
www.cfwebprofessionals.com/blog/general/**battologist**-are-you-one/

Oct 30, 2010 – I was surfing the web this morning, for now I can't remember what – when I ran into the word: **battologist**. It piqued my interest. ...

the **battologist** - YouTube
www.youtube.com/watch?v=hVnW3lSeb2Q

Aug 10, 2010 - 8 min - Uploaded by violettemaschine
Our annual entry into the 48 Hour Film Project-Denver! This was the first year I was director of ...

More videos for **battologist** »

battologist's Music Profile – Users at Last.fm
www.last.fm/user/**battologist**

Figure 10-8

1. Make sure you have an Internet connection by WiFi or cellular signal. Chapter 3 explains how to do that.

2. Open a book and find something about which you want to know more.

3. Follow the rest of the steps according to the kind of tablet you have.

If you have an Apple iPad **iBook app**, follow these steps:

4. Tap the search icon (a magnifying glass).

5. Type your search word, name, or phrase.

6. Tap the Google or the Wikipedia button (usually at the bottom of the search results). See Figure 10-9. The iBook app will close.

7. Tap the results you are looking for.

8. When you are done looking at outside sources, close the browser.

9. Tap the iBooks icon. Your eBook opens to the same page you were on.

Follow these steps if you have a different app, including **Amazon Kindle**, **NOOK**, or **Kobo**:

4. Close the reading app.

5. Tap the Web browser icon on your tablet's home screen.

6. After you have done your research, close the browser.

7. Tap the book app icon to go back to reading your eBook.

Understanding page numbering

Assume one person in your book club has the hardcover, someone else has the paperback edition, and six members have different electronic reading devices, including tablets. No two pages in the room would look alike.

When a sentence reaches the end of the allotted space on the page, it wraps around to the next line. If the hardcover edition has pages that are about six inches wide by nine inches tall, while the paperback edition has pages that are about four inches wide by seven inches tall, something has to give. A sentence that shows up on page 100 of the hardcover might be on page 128 of the paperback.

When it comes to eBooks, add the wonderful ability to choose the type size and style. Start with the fact that a sentence might appear on page 100 of a hardcover. The same sentence might appear 194 pages into an eBook that uses a normal-sized serif typeface — or 527 pages in if you have customized your tablet to use a bold sans-serifs typeface in extra-extra large size. Not everyone's page 128 will have the same text, but the ability to search your tablet's eBooks will come in handy.

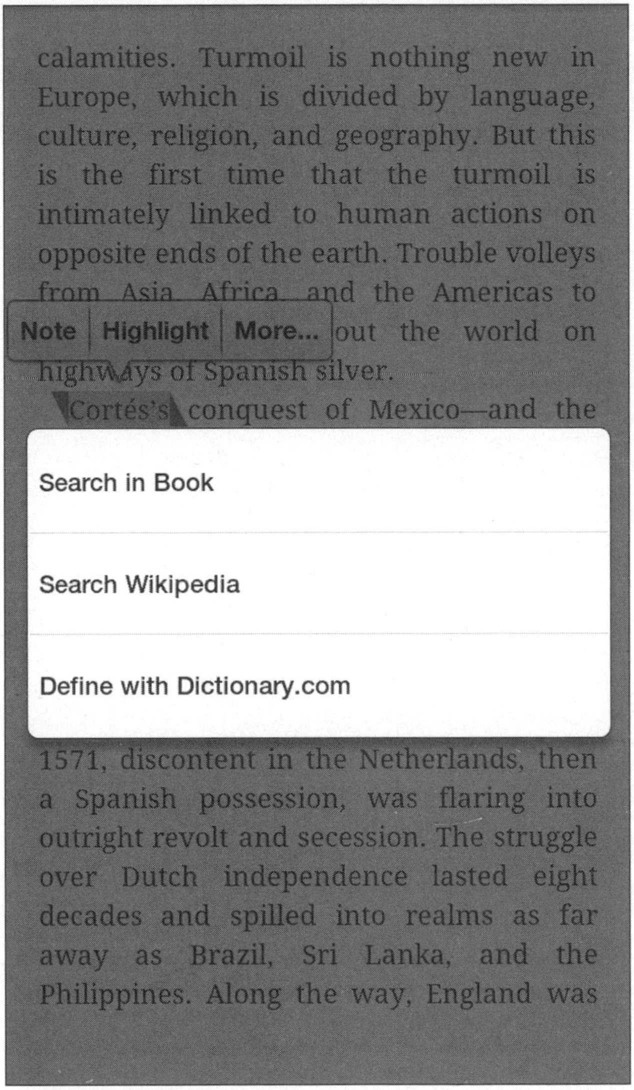

calamities. Turmoil is nothing new in Europe, which is divided by language, culture, religion, and geography. But this is the first time that the turmoil is intimately linked to human actions on opposite ends of the earth. Trouble volleys from Asia, Africa, and the Americas to [Note | Highlight | More...] out the world on highways of Spanish silver.

Cortés's conquest of Mexico—and the

Search in Book

Search Wikipedia

Define with Dictionary.com

1571, discontent in the Netherlands, then a Spanish possession, was flaring into outright revolt and secession. The struggle over Dutch independence lasted eight decades and spilled into realms as far away as Brazil, Sri Lanka, and the Philippines. Along the way, England was

Figure 10-9

Task 6: Changing Text Size and Style

I'll spare you jokes about far-sightedness. Right to the point (size): You can set your own type size on most current eBooks. Depending on your tablet, you may see type in relative terms, kind of like t-shirt sizes: small, medium, normal, large, and extra large. See Figure 10-10. You may also be able choose a point size for the type. Most print books that you read are set in 10-point type.

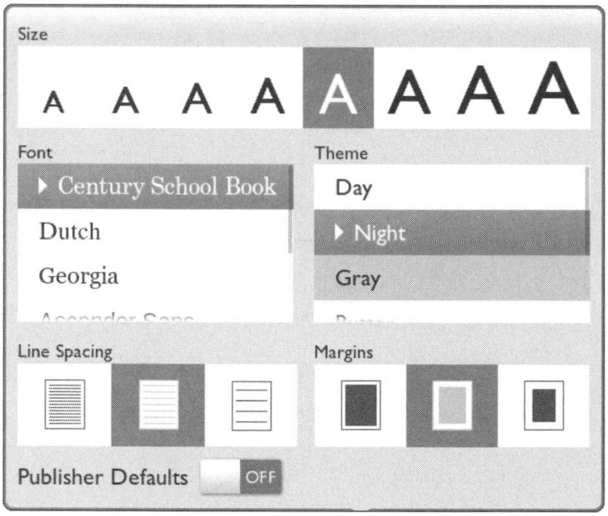

Figure 10-10

Figure 10-11 compares sizes for a typical tablet. As you can see, not only does the typeface change size, but the number of characters that can fit in a line changes. Large type means larger characters, fewer words on the page, and more frequent page turns. Small type means smaller characters, more words on the page, and less frequent page turns.

Small: This line of important text is set in an 8-point typeface

Medium: This line of important text is set in a 9-point typeface

Normal: This line of important text is set in a 10-point typeface

Large: This line of important text is set in an 11-point typeface

Extra-large: This line of important text is set in a 12-point typeface

Figure 10-11

For many books you can choose between one or more styles for the text. The principal distinction here is between serif and sans-serif styles. Serifs are those marks at the left and right side of the horizontal arm at the top of the T, or the extra bits at top and bottom of the vertical stem of the B. The other major class of type is sans serif. Sans-serif type has no serifs.

This short paragraph is set in sans-serif type. As you can see, the letters T and B and all of the others are plain and simple. The other paragraphs above and below use a serif typeface.

Which style is better? What's the best color for your next new car? It's a matter of personal choice. Your choice.

Here's how to choose a type style (typeface) and its size:

1. Open a book on the tablet and go the first page.
2. Tap the Fonts or Typeface or other, similar, button.
3. Follow the rest of the steps according to the kind of tablet you have.

If you have an **Apple iPad**, follow these steps:

4. Tap the AA button in the upper-right corner of the page.
5. Tap the uppercase A to increase the size. It increases each time you tap it. Tap the lowercase a to decrease the size.
6. Tap the Fonts button to change the typeface.
7. Tap a typeface:
   - Baskerville
   - Georgia
   - Palatino
   - Times New Roman
   - Verdana

If you have the **Kobo app** on the **BlackBerry PlayBook**, follow these steps:

4. Swipe down from the top of the tablet's frame.
5. Tap the settings icon. The icon looks like a gear.
6. To change the size of the type, press and hold the marker in the Font Size slider. Move the marker right to increase the size. Move it left to reduce the size.
7. Tap the downward-facing arrow next to the Font Style button to change the typeface.
8. Tap Sans Serif or Serif.

If you have the **Kobo app** on a different kind of tablet, follow these steps:

4. Tap the menu button. The button may be on the tablet's frame (on the Samsung Galaxy Tab) or in a screen. The menu button looks like what you see to the left.
5. Tap the settings icon. It looks like a gear.
6. To change the size of the type, press and hold the marker in the Font Size slider. Move the marker right to increase the size. Move it left to reduce the size.
7. Tap the downward-facing arrow next to the Font Style button to change the typeface.
8. Tap Sans Serif or Serif.

If you have a **Samsung Galaxy Tab**, follow these steps:

1. Press the menu button on the tablet's frame (not the menu icon on the screen). The menu button looks like what you see to the left.
2. Tap View Options.

If you have another version of the **Kindle app**, follow these directions:

1. Tap the menu icon.
2. Tap View Options.
3. Tap the Aa icon.
4. Tap the larger or smaller icon. The text size increases or decreases as you tap the icons.
5. Tap the typeface you want to use, if that option is there. You may not see an option to change the type style.

Color backgrounds

The Kindle app also lets you choose a background color. I like to choose White, so the black text looks more like the newspapers with which I am so familiar. But sometimes, sepia's dark brown type against a light brown background is a soothing combination. When I'm feeling up for a challenge, I make the background black and the text white.

Task 7: Adding Bookmarks, Highlights, or Notes

How can you place a bookmark in a book that does not exist on paper? Use your tablet's special powers. You can place an electronic bookmark, with notes if you want to add them. Also, you can look for the bookmarks you've placed and see your notes. You can see a bookmark I made in Figure 10-12. It's also highlighted.

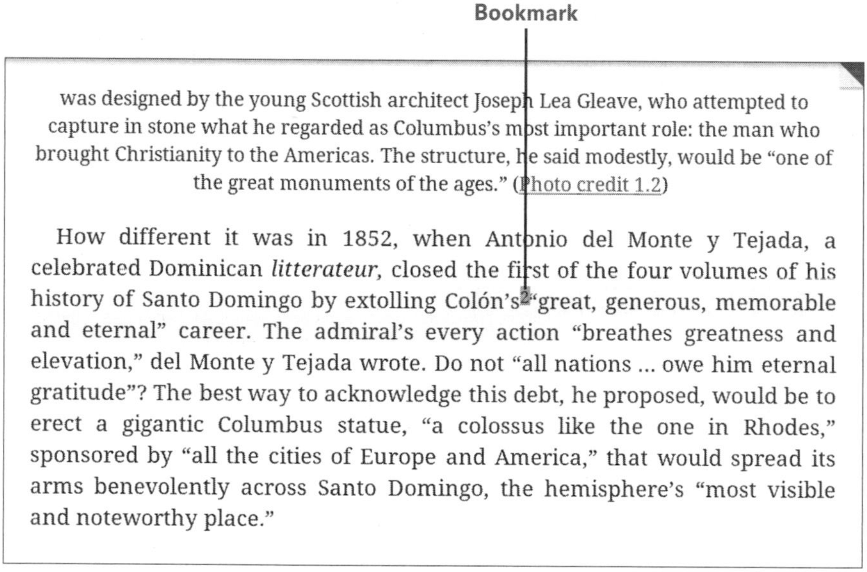

Bookmark

was designed by the young Scottish architect Joseph Lea Gleave, who attempted to capture in stone what he regarded as Columbus's most important role: the man who brought Christianity to the Americas. The structure, he said modestly, would be "one of the great monuments of the ages." (Photo credit 1.2)

How different it was in 1852, when Antonio del Monte y Tejada, a celebrated Dominican *litterateur,* closed the first of the four volumes of his history of Santo Domingo by extolling Colón's great, generous, memorable and eternal" career. The admiral's every action "breathes greatness and elevation," del Monte y Tejada wrote. Do not "all nations ... owe him eternal gratitude"? The best way to acknowledge this debt, he proposed, would be to erect a gigantic Columbus statue, "a colossus like the one in Rhodes," sponsored by "all the cities of Europe and America," that would spread its arms benevolently across Santo Domingo, the hemisphere's "most visible and noteworthy place."

Figure 10-12

Here's how to add a bookmark:

1. Open an eBook, start reading, and find something you want to remember.
2. Follow the rest of the steps according to the kind of tablet you have.

If you have an **Apple iPad**, follow these steps:

3. Tap the bookmark icon near the upper-right corner of screen. If you change your mind, tap the ribbon to remove it.
4. To add a highlighting color, touch and hold your finger on a word. Drag the highlighting color to expand the area.
5. Tap Bookmark.

If you have the **Kobo app** on a **BlackBerry PlayBook** or other tablet, do this:

3. Tap in the upper-right corner of the page.

If you have the **Kindle app** on the **Samsung Galaxy Tab** or another tablet, follow these steps:

3. Tap the upper-right corner of the screen. Tap again if you change your mind.
4. To add a note, press and hold on the text.
5. Tap Note.
6. Type your note.

Task 8: Finding a Bookmark or Note

You're a bookmarking fool. You've placed them through the eBook. Isn't it great that you don't have to worry about them falling out? How do you jump to any or all of them? You can see all my bookmarks in Figure 10-13.

Here's how:

1. Open an eBook on the screen.
2. Follow the remaining steps depending on the kind of tablet you have.

If you have an **Apple iPad**, follow these steps:

3. Tap the Table of Contents/Bookmark button.
4. Tap Bookmarks. You'll see a list of your bookmarks, along with the chapter, page, date you marked it, and a phrase or two of surrounding text.
5. Tap the bookmark you want to go to. To go back to bookmarks, tap outside the bookmark.

If you have a **Kobo app** on the **BlackBerry PlayBook**, follow these steps:

3. Swipe down from the tablet's top frame.
4. Tap the Dogears button.
5. Tap the bookmark you want to go to.

If you have the **Kobo app** on another tablet, follow these directions:

1. Tap the menu button to display available options.
2. Tap the Dogears button.
3. Tap the bookmark you want to go to.

If you have a **Samsung Galaxy Tab**, follow these steps:

1. Press the menu button on the tablet's frame (not the menu icon on the screen). The menu button looks like what you see to the left.
2. Tap the Go To button.
3. Tap My Notes & Marks. On other versions of the Kindle app, display the menu and then tap the Go To button.
4. Tap the bookmark you want to go to.

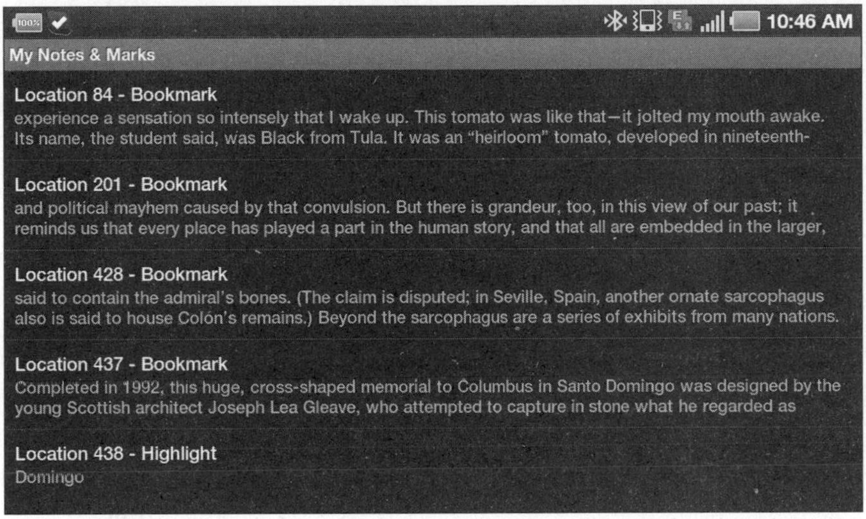

My Notes & Marks

Location 84 - Bookmark
experience a sensation so intensely that I wake up. This tomato was like that—it jolted my mouth awake. Its name, the student said, was Black from Tula. It was an "heirloom" tomato, developed in nineteenth-

Location 201 - Bookmark
and political mayhem caused by that convulsion. But there is grandeur, too, in this view of our past; it reminds us that every place has played a part in the human story, and that all are embedded in the larger,

Location 428 - Bookmark
said to contain the admiral's bones. (The claim is disputed; in Seville, Spain, another ornate sarcophagus also is said to house Colón's remains.) Beyond the sarcophagus are a series of exhibits from many nations.

Location 437 - Bookmark
Completed in 1992, this huge, cross-shaped memorial to Columbus in Santo Domingo was designed by the young Scottish architect Joseph Lea Gleave, who attempted to capture in stone what he regarded as

Location 438 - Highlight
Domingo

Figure 10-13

Chapter 11

Finding eBooks and Other Reading Materials

Attention lounge lizards: Not only can you read eBooks in your Dr. Denton's, but you can also visit the bookstore in your PJs . . . or less. Me? I love browsing for real books in a real bookstore; I almost always come away with something unexpected. On the other hand, the convenience of shopping for an eBook from my tablet's screen is just about unbeatable. It is near-instant gratification without moving the car, picking up packages from the mailbox, or putting on shoes.

tech to connect

activities

- Task 1: Buying eBooks
- Task 2: Finding Free eBooks
- Task 3: Getting Newspapers and Magazines
- Task 4: Borrowing from the Library
- Task 5: Adding Your Own Files

Task 1: Buying eBooks

Every major tablet maker has a bookstore app. Some tablets (like the BlackBerry PlayBook) have an app from Kobo instead. The Toshiba Thrive (an Android-based tablet) has a store called Toshiba Book Place. Figure 11-1 shows a wise selection I'm about to make from the Amazon store. AARP has its own bookstore at `aarp.org/bookstore`.

But you can buy from other places besides an official store. You can run an Amazon Kindle app on an Apple iPad, Samsung, or BlackBerry PlayBook. You can add the NOOK or the Kobo apps.

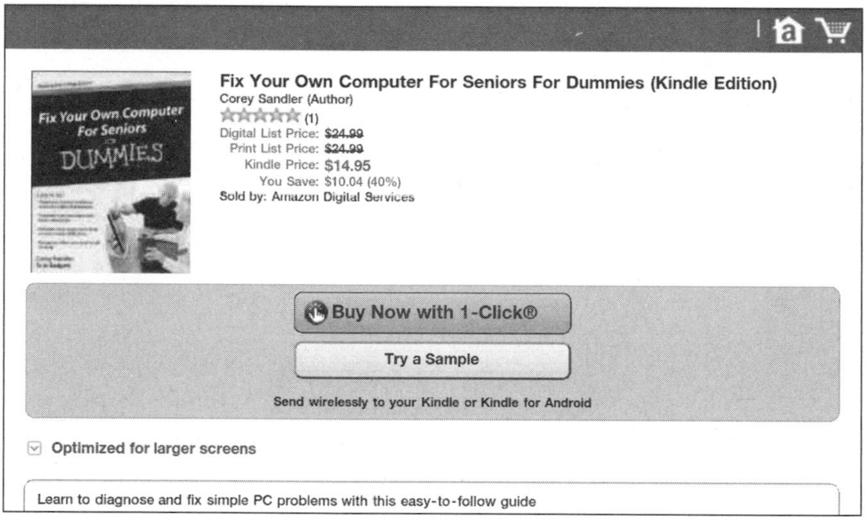

Fix Your Own Computer For Seniors For Dummies (Kindle Edition)
Corey Sandler (Author)
⭐⭐⭐⭐⭐ (1)
Digital List Price: ~~$24.99~~
Print List Price: ~~$24.99~~
Kindle Price: $14.95
You Save: $10.04 (40%)
Sold by: Amazon Digital Services

Buy Now with 1-Click®

Try a Sample

Send wirelessly to your Kindle or Kindle for Android

☑ Optimized for larger screens

Learn to diagnose and fix simple PC problems with this easy-to-follow guide

Figure 11-1

The following steps assume you have signed up for an account with the store or app you're using. That is a necessary step, for it is how online sellers charge your credit card (which you also have to provide). Signing up will involve steps that are much like what you see in Chapter 8, "Watching Videos and Movies." In that chapter I take you through the signup for a Netflix account.

Usually the book publisher (not the store) sets the price for books, which means there isn't much comparison shopping to be done. However, watch your email for Internet coupons and special offers. They'll start after you sign up for the store account.

Here is a general guide to shopping and purchasing:

1. Make sure you have a WiFi or cellular Internet connection. Chapter 3 tells you how to do that.

2. Tap the store or app icon on your tablet's home screen.

3. Browse the offerings. To search instead of browse, tap in the box labeled Search. Type what you know: author, title, or ISBN. You may be able to look by genre: fiction, literature, biography, romance, mystery, history, business, sports, or travel. See Figure 11-2.

4. Tap a book cover if you want to read
   - A summary of the book
   - The table of contents or index
   - Reviews by professional critics or amateur readers
   - An online sample of the book

5. Tap Buy. You will see a purchase on your next credit card bill. You're charged on the credit card whose information you entered when you signed up for a store/app account.

6. The eBook will be put on your tablet. For what to do to start reading, refer to this book's Chapter 10.

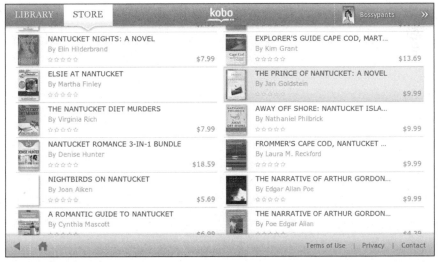

Figure 11-2

Online bookstores know what they have sold to you. If you accidentally delete an eBook, get in touch with the place where you bought it. In general, your eBooks are linked to your account (rather than to a specific tablet). Read the help section or FAQ (frequently asked questions) to see about getting your eBook back.

Security clearance

Should you include your credit card number in your online bookstore account? Some stores don't give you a choice, but others do. Although it may sound risky to include your credit card, if you think about it, that information is already recorded in many places. You use your credit card at brick-and-mortar stores, restaurants, and online shoe stores. Any one of them could end up the target of a thief. Use these very important defenses: Always use a complex and unguessable password. Regularly check your credit card statements. Immediately notify the card issuer if you see a charge you do not recognize. Doing so gives you the protection of federal law against unauthorized charges.

Task 2: Finding Free eBooks

You can find plenty of great free reads from authors who no longer need the money:

- `books.google.com` is Google Books, which presents a collection of classic and obscure books. Some are in plain type, some are just scans (pictures) of pages, and some are EPUB files that can go right onto your tablet. See Figure 11-3.
- `Feedbooks.com` specializes in 19th-century classics. This site also offers EPUB downloads that can be directly loaded onto your eReader.
- `Gutenberg.org` is the home of Project Gutenberg. The eBooks that are in PDF or EPUB format can most likely work on your tablet. See Figure 11-4.
- `Manybooks.net` has a combination of some of the same books you'll find on Project Gutenberg along with some new work by current authors in search of an audience.

The beauty of using a site like Project Gutenberg is that you don't need an account. Even better, you don't need to pay any money. That is, unless you contribute to the people who are converting out-of-copyright classics and old titles into digital form.

To use Project Gutenberg, do the following:

1. Make sure your tablet has a connection to the web. Chapter 3 tells you how to make sure of that.
2. Tap the web browser icon, tap in the address box, and type `gutenberg.org`. (Remember: The address ends in .org, not .com, like so many sites.)
3. Type a book title, author, or category in the search box.
4. Tap Download This eBook when you find a book you want. Titles usually come in different formats. Choose EPUB. (Choose Kindle if you are using the Kindle app.) You can experiment with several different formats to find the one that works best on your tablet.

Figure 11-3

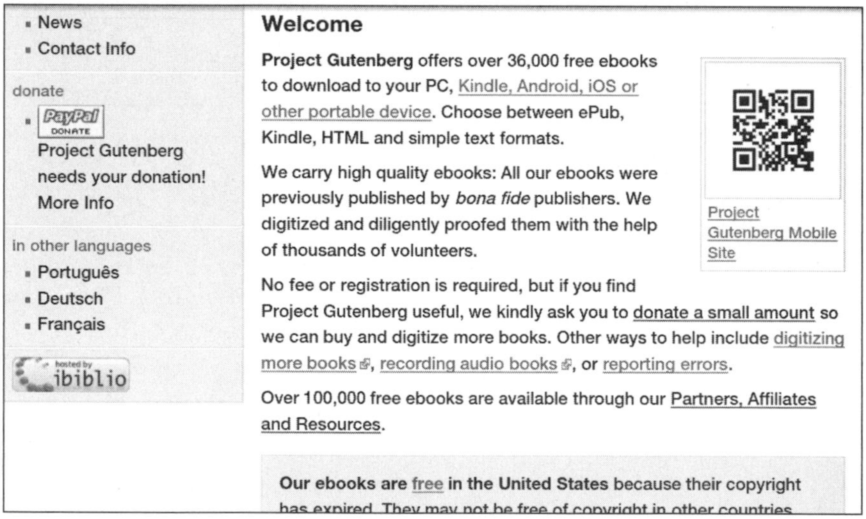

News
Contact Info

donate
PayPal DONATE
Project Gutenberg
needs your donation!
More Info

in other languages
Português
Deutsch
Français

hosted by ibiblio

Welcome

Project Gutenberg offers over 36,000 free ebooks
to download to your PC, Kindle, Android, iOS or
other portable device. Choose between ePub,
Kindle, HTML and simple text formats.

We carry high quality ebooks: All our ebooks were
previously published by *bona fide* publishers. We
digitized and diligently proofed them with the help
of thousands of volunteers.

Project
Gutenberg Mobile
Site

No fee or registration is required, but if you find
Project Gutenberg useful, we kindly ask you to donate a small amount so
we can buy and digitize more books. Other ways to help include digitizing
more books, recording audio books, or reporting errors.

Over 100,000 free ebooks are available through our Partners, Affiliates
and Resources.

Our ebooks are free in the United States because their copyright
has expired. They may not be free of copyright in other countries.

Figure 11-4

Task 3: Getting Newspapers and Magazines

Your tablet doesn't just handle eBooks. It also lets you read newspapers and magazines, like the one you see in Figure 11-5. And on tablets that show color, you can read comic books and colorful children's books (to the grandkids, I'm assuming).

Figure 11-5

Tough NYTimes

I spent two decades of my life directly involved in the newspaper and magazine business. I began as a newsboy delivering papers by bicycle. I was an editor of my high school and college newspapers. I worked my way through graduate school as a printer. After that I was a reporter for two daily newspapers and a correspondent for The Associated Press. I also was editor of two national magazines. And now, more than four decades after graduation from college, I still start my day reading *The New York Times* and often two or three other newspapers. Only now I no longer can smell the ink or feel it on my hands. It is hard to tell if newspapers as we know them will survive much longer. But one possible salvation is to get people in the habit of paying for online access to first-class journalism. It's a tough slog; most people are used to getting "news" for what they believe to be free by watching the television networks. To me, TV news (and much of the rest of its offerings) is insubstantial fluff.

Periodicals come in two types. Some are made specifically for tablets, and their electronic version is the same as the print edition. These editions are usually sent to your tablet after you subscribe. Some are online versions of publications available at websites. Most of the time they are separate from the print version. You can get these editions any time you visit the site from your tablet.

The following steps assume you have signed up for an account with the bookstore. If you haven't, do that first, and then come back here. Chapter 8 tells you how to sign up for a membership to Netflix, and the process is much the same. Be prepared to give your credit card information so you can actually pay for what you're buying. Also, some subscriptions come to you by cellular data. Make sure you know the policies so you are not surprised with a large bill from your cellular provider.

Most publications let you choose between a single issue and a less-expensive annual subscription (usually billed monthly). If you choose a subscription, later you can go to the same page and tap Unsubscribe to end your financial obligation to the publisher.

Here's how to subscribe to a newspaper or magazine made specifically for a tablet:

1. Tap the bookstore app icon.
2. Browse the offerings.
3. Tap Subscribe. Your credit card will be billed. The first issue should show up on your tablet within minutes. Subsequent issues arrive automatically, on the publication's schedule: Monthly magazines show up once a month, weeklies once a week, and dailies usually overnight so that you can read them at breakfast (careful with the cup of coffee) or on your commute. If your tablet is off, the next issue will show up the next time it gets a chance. See Figure 11-6.

Most online newsstands automatically archive older editions. On the newspaper's website, tap Help (or the like) and read the pages. You should be able to get most publications from the archive.

Different periodicals offer different options in terms of free and paid content. Here's what you may find:

- Free access to an online version of the current printed edition
- Free access to a limited version of the current edition
- A button you can tap to buy the current edition or to subscribe; see Figure 11-7

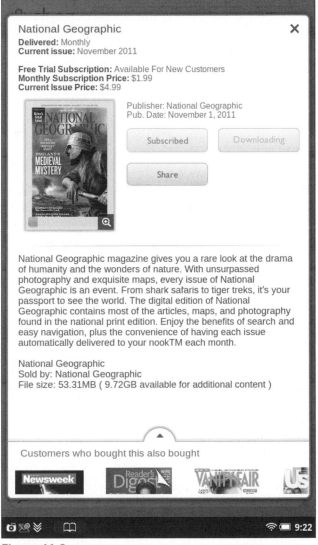

Figure 11-6

Here's how to use a web version of a publication:

1. Turn on your tablet and make sure you have a wireless connection to the Internet. Chapter 3 tells how to do that.
2. Tap your tablet's web browser icon.

3. Tap in the address box and type the newspaper's or magazine's address. If you don't know the address, type the title in a search engine such as Google or Bing.

4. Read. You will see the latest edition when you visit the publisher's website. Some subscriptions let you search through archives. Subscribers to *The New York Times*, for example, can search archives that date back to 1851.

Tap to buy

Figure 11-7

If you already subscribe to the print version of a publication, see if you can get a free or reduced-price subscription to the online edition.

Task 4: Borrowing from the Library

When I was a kid, one of my favorite places to lurk after school was the public library. Books old and new, magazines popular and obscure, and newspapers from around the world. I even developed a crush or two on a few of the librarians; I'd like to think they at least noticed me. Now, though, the library can also come to me.

Libraries around the country are allowed to loan some of their titles as eBooks. With the tap of a finger, you can borrow the file for a book. See Figure 11-8. Most libraries allow loan of a limited number of titles at one time, and for a specific time period usually of one or two weeks.

tech tip

Not every digital version of a book is available for library loan. Thank you for your patronage.

Nantucket Atheneum

I live in a place with an iconic library. The great Nantucket Atheneum, a Greek Revival masterpiece built in 1847, is now a national historic landmark. I've spent months inhaling the dust from arcane books collected for the whaleship owners and crews; I've studied current titles as well, sitting in the hall where Frederick Douglass, Ralph Waldo Emerson, Henry David Thoreau, Lucretia Mott, and many others came to give lectures.

The Atheneum leverages its resources by membership in a regional association of libraries that includes 32 libraries on Cape Cod, Nantucket, and Martha's Vineyard; they're bound together in the oh-so-cutely named CLAMS (Cape Libraries Automated Materials Sharing) group. Cardholders from any one of the libraries can borrow available titles from any collection in CLAMS.

Figure 11-8

Most libraries use either Adobe Digital Editions or the Overdrive Media Console. Adobe Digital Editions is shown in Figure 11-9. Here's how a typical library loan works:

1. Visit the website for your library of choice. You need a valid library card, which may require a visit to the institution itself.

2. Read the instructions from the library about how to use digital materials.

3. Confirm whether your tablet is listed as a device that can read the library's eBooks. Most tablets are supported.

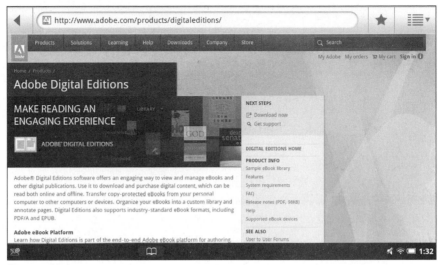

Figure 11-9

4. Download the library's app on your tablet or computer. These apps prevent unauthorized copying and impose a time limit on the loan.

5. Browse through the library's titles.

6. Tap a book that's available for immediate loan. If you see a book that you want to read but is already out on loan, you can (usually) place a hold on the book. My wish list is in Figure 11-10.

7. Go to your cart and tap Download. The eBook is sent to your device. You don't need to do anything else.

8. Tap your tablet's reading app to find the book. Depending on the way the library has set up its lending system, you may find the book through the Overdrive Media Console or through a Kindle or Kobo or other reading app.

9. Tap the book cover and begin your literary perusal.

If your tablet is not directly supported by the library, try this instead:

1. Download a free program that works on your desktop or laptop computer. Don't try to download it to your tablet. You should see the program on the library's website.

2. Read and follow the instructions that came with the program. You may be asked to download an encrypted copy of the book file directly from the library's website to your computer, or you may be asked to do the same thing from within the program on your computer.

3. After the eBook is on your computer, turn on your tablet.

4. Plug your USB cord into your tablet. Careful! Specific instructions are in Chapter 3. You are officially getting ready to side load files.

5. Plug the other end of the USB cable into your computer.

6. You may need to authorize your tablet. Just respond to the onscreen query that asks for your library card or for your tablet's ID.

7. Drag and drop the book title from the window that represents your computer to the window that represents your tablet.

Figure 11-10

Task 5: Adding Your Own Files

You can easily copy some of your personal files — the novel you're working on, your budget spreadsheets, the photos from your latest vacation — from a computer to your tablet. When you get the files on your tablet, you can read them just as pretty as you please.

Here's how to process and transfer personal files to your tablet:

1. Do any editing and formatting on your desktop or laptop computer. It takes a bit of experimentation and practice, but try not to pack a huge amount of small type into a large page. Consider your tablet's size and shape.
2. Copy the file with a new name.
3. Choose File and then choose Save As.
4. From the Save As Type menu, select the format that goes with your document:
    - Text files. Most tablets can use DOC, DOCX, and TXT.
    - Spreadsheets. Save the file as either an XLS or XLSX.
    - Photos and drawings. Most tablets can use JPG or PNG.
    - Various files. Save text, spreadsheet, and image files as PDFs if possible.
5. Plug the USB cable into your tablet and your computer. See Figure 11-11. Careful there! Chapter 3 has directions for what you're doing, which is side loading files. If you'd rather, attach the document to an email that you send to your tablet.
6. Find the files on your tablet. Tap My Files (or something with a similar name). You should see photos in a gallery or pictures app.
7. Tap any file name or icon to open it on your tablet.

No moss

When I travel, I regularly add these things to my tablet:

Travel documents, including itineraries, airline e-tickets, hotel confirmations, and a text or PDF version of my calendar

Notes for presentations or lectures

Shopping lists (and I can use the web to research prices and locations while I travel)

Personal photos or documents. You never know when you'll have a captive audience to show pictures of the kids and grandkids, or a selection from your collection of Elvis photos.

Pinch in or out to adjust the display. It may be easier to read documents by turning the tablet sideways.

Plug into
tablet

Plug into desktop
or laptop computer

Figure 11-11

Chapter 12

Understanding Technicalities

Although we may think of our wondrous devices as magic tablets, in truth the Apple iPad, the BlackBerry PlayBook, the NOOK Tablet, and the whole panoply of Android-based devices are actually downsized but still wondrously capable computers.

In this section, I'll deal with a few essential elements of technical operations. Don't worry, though: You don't need a soldering iron or slide rule. We'll deal here with things like the art and science of choosing a password and the best way to use your battery. Then you go shopping for new apps that extend, expand, and otherwise personalize your tablet.

tech to connect

activities

- Task 1: Understanding Warranties
- Task 2: Managing Battery Power
- Task 3: Reawakening a Dead Tablet
- Task 4: Choosing a Password
- Task 5: Finding New Apps
- Task 6: Downloading New Apps
- Task 7: Cleaning Your Touchscreen
- Task 8: Organizing Your Home Screen
- Task 9: Updating the Operating System

Task 1: Understanding Warranties

Whatever you do, follow the terms of the manufacturer's warranty. Most warranties do not cover damage to your tablet caused by water or a tumble to the floor. You'll also be warned against opening up the sealed case or performing other modifications to the device. I also suggest keeping your tablet out of reach of the family dog, away from the stove, and safely in its case during hailstorms.

Here are the steps you should do when you first buy a tablet:

1. Keep a copy of the sales receipt and other paperwork. If for some reason you lose them, most retailers will give you a copy.

2. Register your tablet with the manufacturer when you set it up the first time. Most tablets will insist you do this the first time you turn them on. You'll be asked for your name, address, and email address. Registration protects your warranty rights. It also helps make sure you know about (or just plain old get unbeknownst to you) any tablet updates.

3. Read the warranty. You should know the following:
   - How long is your warranty in effect?
   - What is excluded?

Should you buy an extended warranty?

Some manufacturers or stores will try to sell you an extended warranty that covers your tablet for a longer period than the basic guarantee. Before you spend the money, analyze the basic warranty. If the warranty is only good for a very short period of time, and if the terms are unreasonably limited, be cautious about buying their product, period.

How much does it cost to buy the extended warranty? If the price is high, maybe it makes more sense to put aside that amount of money in a savings account. Then, you can be prepared to either pay for repairs or use the money to buy a new tablet after a year or so. Technology is always improving; prices are always dropping.

And finally, consider buying the tablet with a credit card that offers a buyer protection or extended warranty plan as part of its regular benefits. Some credit cards add a year's coverage to anything you buy. I've used this feature several times in supporting my children's purchases: One was burgled and one unexpectedly saw the demise of an electronic device.

Task 2: Managing Battery Power

Modern rechargeable batteries have almost nothing in common with the big, weak cells we used to power a flashlight. Modern batteries are small, powerful, and smart, and it will help to know how to get the most out of them.

Modern rechargeable batteries get warm when you use them. Warm — but not fry-an-egg hot. If you think the battery is too hot, or is otherwise acting odd, turn off your tablet. Then get in touch with the manufacturer before you use it again.

Here are the basic rules of power:

- Charge your battery completely before you use it the first time. Recharge the battery fully every time after.
- Read the owner's manual before you recharge the battery. Most tablets can be recharged simply by plugging in the power adapter, which connects to an AC source; some tablets have to be turned on.
- Don't let the battery run completely out of juice. See Figure 12-1. Turn off the tablet when you see the low charge alert.
- Avoid extremely high or low temperatures, whether you're using, recharging, or storing your battery. That means it probably does not make sense to read a book while riding a ski lift or while perched atop an elephant on photo safari in Kenya.
- Recharge the battery before putting the tablet on the shelf for a long time. If you plan to put your tablet away for a few weeks or more, charge the battery fully and turn off the tablet completely.

- If the battery fails, send it in for repair. Don't try to replace or repair anything yourself. Doing so will probably void the warranty.

Battery you have left

100%		⌗□ .ıl ▭ 1:44 PM
Unplugged for 3m 47s		
☀ Display		88%
⊙ Android System		7%
℗ Photoshop Express		3%
▶ Gallery		2%

Figure 12-1

Task 3: Reawakening a Dead Tablet

In some cases a tablet just won't respond properly.

If your tablet starts acting squirrely, you might try these courses of action:

1. Check the battery level. On the home screen you can see how much juice it has left. See Figure 12-2.
2. Close an app or two if you aren't using them.
3. Make sure your recharger is getting power. Make sure it is plugged into a live outlet. If the charger is attached to a power strip, make sure that device is on.

Figure 12-2

Time and a half

I'm pretty advanced when it comes to technical matters, but I do have a confession to make: I once paid good money to a washing machine repair technician to learn that the machine was not performing properly because the water faucet was turned off.

Task 4: Choosing a Password

Why should you use a password for any website that involves your personal, financial, or otherwise private information and preferences? Because, alas, the world is crawling with creeps who have moved on from picking pockets or grabbing handbags to the electronic equivalent: hacking into online computer accounts.

You should do three basic things to protect yourself:

- Only reveal what needs to be shown to others. Always assume that any photo, writing, or private information might someday be revealed to a would-be evildoer. Assume that postings to social networks, answers to surveys, or other such data are forever.
- Closely watch your banking, credit card, investment, and other accounts. Look for possible fraud. If you see any, immediately notify the institution and change passwords and accounts. See Figure 12-3.
- Create a strong password for any site that holds personal information, and make changes to it from time to time. See Figure 12-4.

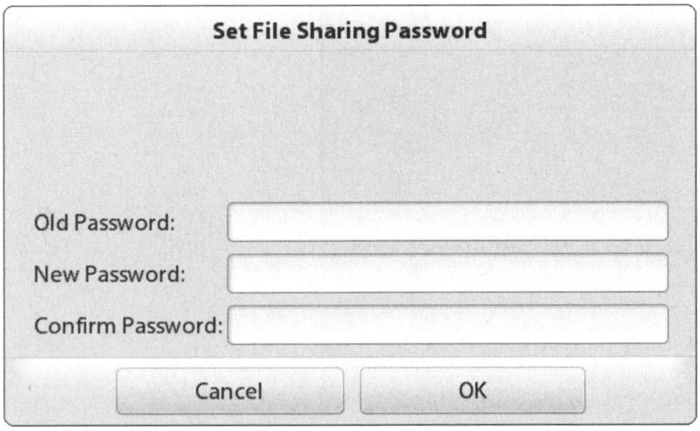

Set File Sharing Password

Old Password:

New Password:

Confirm Password:

Cancel   OK

Figure 12-3

Figure 12-4

Here is how you make a strong password:

 Avoid the obvious. Don't use something that anyone with just a bit of research could easily find: your birthday, the name of your significant other, or your local sports team.

■ Choose a password that is not in any way directly linked to you. I'm going to reveal here one of my favorites: I pick a telephone number of a store or a restaurant or a business from the phone book. There is nothing that would make a hacker guess that I am using the number for a dry cleaner two towns over; and I know that if I forget that number I can always look it up in the phone book.

■ Make the password more complex by adding a word or phrase to the number you chose. Preface the number with the name of your favorite far-away vacation spot.

■ Never give your password to someone who calls you or sends you an email and requests it — even if the email looks like it came directly from your bank (or credit card company, or whatever). If such people truly work for the bank or the credit card company, they already have any information they need; an unexpected call is quite possibly a scam.

Task 5: Finding New Apps

Applications — apps — are small programs that add new features to a tablet. Apps include so many examples: a program that crops and adjusts photo colors, a program that adds social networking (like Facebook or Twitter); a program that can find WiFi systems as you move about town. Most intriguingly, apps can offer to do things that none of us even considered when we first bought a tablet. You can see the Android app store in Figure 12-5.

You have to use apps that are designed for your particular tablet (or in some cases, for the particular model and operating system). An app that was developed for the Apple iPad will not work on the BlackBerry PlayBook, for example.

Try these spots to find apps:

- The Internet store that is run by the company that made your tablet. When you get an app from here, you know it will work with your tablet.

- The Internet store that is run by the company that makes your tablet's operating system (not the machine itself, but the main program that your tablet uses). The store should be able to tell which version you are using (without your help), but you might have to identify the brand and model.

- The Internet store that is run by the company that provides your tablet's cellular connection. (This assumes your tablet has a cellular data radio.) For example, T-Mobile or Sprint may offer an app store for its clients.

- Any other company that offers apps for a variety of devices and operating systems. Amazon is an example of such a company.

- Any other app maker. Your bank, for example, may have an app so you can bank online.

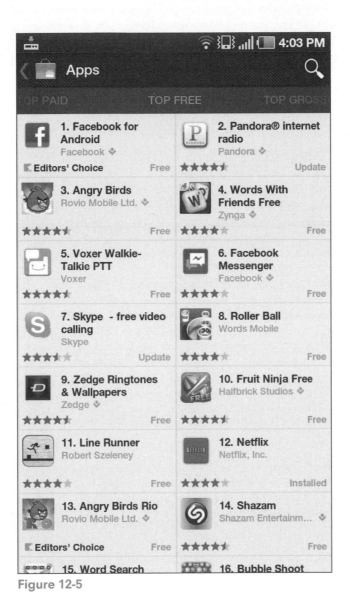

Figure 12-5

Task 6: Downloading New Apps

Before you go out in search of fun new apps, make sure the following bases are covered:

1. Write down this information about your tablet:
   - Manufacturer (Apple, Samsung, and Research in Motion [RIM] are examples)
   - Model name (BlackBerry PlayBook and NOOK Tablet are examples)
   - Operating system (OS 2.0 for the BlackBerry, or iOS 5.0 for an iPad for example)

   Most of this information should be on the box the tablet came in. If not, check the device itself. For example, on most Android-based tablets, tap Settings, and then tap About Tablet.

2. Make sure your tablet is properly registered with the manufacturer. You can register when you set it up for the first time; in fact, most tablet makers won't let you begin using the device until you register it with them.

3. Make sure your tablet has a wireless connection to the Internet. In most situations, you want to use WiFi. It is usually cheaper and faster than a cellular data link. Chapter 3 tells you how to set up an Internet connection.

You can read customer reviews about apps to decide whether one is worth buying (or even downloading, if it is free). When you read an app's description, it will be accompanied by user reviews. Here's a general guide to downloading and installing apps on your tablet:

1. To use an official source, tap the app icon. The icon is on your home screen. Sometimes the icon is named App Store; on others it is named Market or other such commercial name. To use an unofficial source, tap the Web browser icon and type the website address.

2. If this is the first time you have visited the store, you will have to sign up for an account. Type your name, email address, credit card number, and a password. The credit card you enter is billed for any apps you buy. Make the password complex to help protect your credit card.

3. Tap a category. Or, tap in the search box and type a name or kind.

4. Tap an app to read a description and reviews. Figure 12-6 shows an example. You may be able to get a free trial. Some apps are free, in which case your credit card is not charged. Or, there may be a free trial period. Eventually, in that case, you have to either pay for it or delete it.

5. Tap Purchase or Buy or Download.

6. Confirm that you want to buy the app. It starts coming to your tablet automatically after you do that. Most take just a few seconds or minutes to arrive. See Figure 12-7.

7. Once an app has been downloaded, tap its name on the home screen. You might have to set up the app to be able to use it. In the long run, some app developers will send you a message if they have updated (improved) an app you bought. Or, you can go to the store and check for updates. Just tap Update or Upgrade in that case.

Figure 12-6

You can see the app downloading.

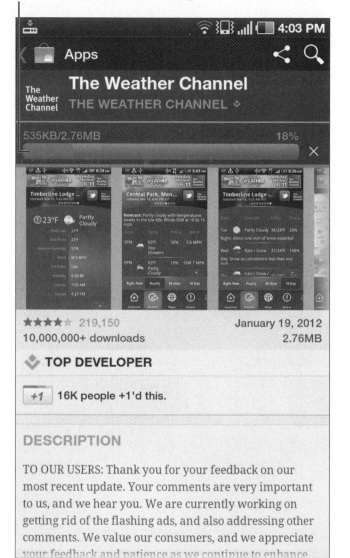

Figure 12-7

Task 7: Cleaning Your Touchscreen

First of all, I need to make an important point of distinction here. There is the process of removing finger prints, smudges of French fry oil, and the other various detritus left behind by humans; I call that cleaning.

The first and most important word of warning: Do not use power tools, bottles of Mr. Clean, or a mop and pail to clean your tablet. You could damage the delicate electronics within. The second word: The top surface of the touchscreen is covered with glass or acrylic and is relatively tough to scratch. But it is not bulletproof. Don't write on its surface with a pen and don't drop heavy objects on it.

You will have to clean your tablet from time to time. Here's how:

1. Turn off the tablet.
2. Gently polish the screen with a soft cloth. Use a cloth like the one you use to clean your eyeglasses. Some tablets come with a polishing cloth.

Oleo oleo scratching free

Some tablets, most notably the Apple iPad, apply a special oleophobic coating to the surface of their screens. (*Oleophobic* is a fancy term from the world of advanced chemistry that strings together the Greek words that literally mean "fear of fat.") In this case it does not refer to a diet plan, but instead to a coating that resists oily buildup from fingertips.

Task 8: Organizing Your Home Screen

Cleaning is not the same as housekeeping. Neatening up icons, shortcuts, and notes on your tablet's home screen: I call that housekeeping. Your tablet probably showed up with things like these: a web browser, an email app where you can handle communication, files, and the way things look.

On most tablets, you can change things so that just a few icons appear on the home screen. A copy of the icon is placed there, and the original icon stays on the screen's secondary page. Read your tablet's instruction manual for the steps. Here is a typical way to copy an icon (create a shortcut) to the home screen:

1. Go to the screen where the icon is displayed. Some tablets organize icons by type (media, communication, apps); some tablets list icons in alphabetical order.
2. Press and hold an icon. Some tablets automatically put the icon on the home screen. Other tablets show you a menu, where you have to tap the option you want.

Most tablets let you rearrange and remove icons. Remember: The icons on the home screen are copies. Getting rid of an icon from the home screen doesn't take the app off your tablet.

Here's how to perform housekeeping:

1. Press and hold an icon. It will probably pulse or flash; keep your finger on the icon. See Figure 12-8.
2. Drag the icon where you want it. To delete the icon, drag it to a Trash or Remove box on the home screen. If you see a menu, tap the Remove option.

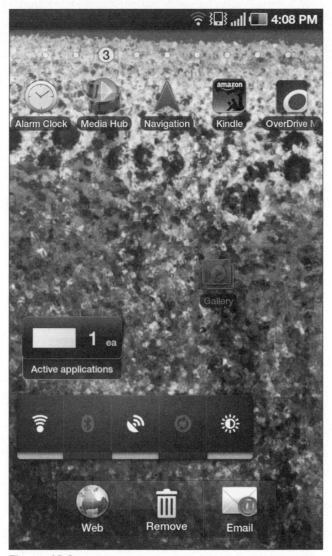

Figure 12-8

Task 9: Updating the Operating System

You can do many a thing to change your tablet. The next step beyond is updating or changing the operating system. The operating system isn't the machine itself, but the main program that your tablet uses.

The operating system probably will need updates over time to fix problems or add features. See Figure 12-9.

Read your tablet's instruction manual for specifics. Here are some common ways to get updates:

- Updates may automatically come to your tablet when you use WiFi or connect to the manufacturer's website. In this case, you don't have to do anything.

- You may get an email telling you to visit a particular site. Make sure the email is from the maker of your tablet. One way to be cautious here is to ignore the incoming message. Instead, go to the Settings panel and tap Update Operating System (or Software Updates or a similar command) and see if there is a new version due to come your way.

- You can go to a page on your tablet and tap a button to see if you have the most updated operating system. To do this, you must be connected to the Internet. See Figure 12-10.

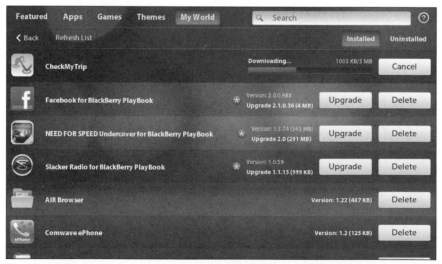

Figure 12-9

A major change can require you to download a file to your personal computer and then side load it across to your tablet on the USB cable. (Chapter 3 explains how to do that.) Read and follow any instructions that appear on the screen or in an email.

Figure 12-10

Chapter 13

Making Things Easier

My new car has more buttons, electronic displays, and settings than the Space Shuttle. Now, I am a pretty technical guy, and I do write books about some of the most arcane details of computers, tablets, and cameras. But I have to admit that when I'm driving, I concentrate most of my attention on a handful of minor details — like the up-to-the-second display of current miles per gallon.

It's the same way with advanced tablets. Every tablet on the market is almost infinitely useful and adaptable. You can use them to browse the web, read books, and send email. And I know you will find having those tasks in the palm of your hand very useful. But many people also find one or two features that provide extra pleasure: a customizable alarm clock, adjustable system sounds, and a security system that would make James Bond think twice about entering without knocking.

activities

tech 2 to connect

- Task 1: Adjusting the Screen
- Task 2: Setting Timeouts
- Task 3: Fixing the Clock
- Task 4: Setting the Alarm
- Task 5: Doing the Math
- Task 6: Converting Numbers
- Task 7: Going to Flight Mode

Task 1: Adjusting the Screen

When I occasionally get angry, or when I watch the Boston baseball team, I see red. (And sometimes the Boston Red Sox make me angry.) But what I can't be sure of is if the red I see is exactly the same as what you see. Luckily, you can adjust your tablet's brightness and color. I find it very satisfying to see an image with rich blacks, bright whites, and electrifying reds and yellows. But that's just me.

Here's how to change your tablet's screen:

1. Tap the settings icon. It may be on the tablet's home screen and called Settings, or you may have to swipe down from the frame.

2. Tap Display Settings (or Screen, or another similar tool name).

3. Tap the available adjustments. See Figure 13-1. See how they change, just one at a time. Adjust the settings by touching and dragging the slider.

4. Adjust the Brightness setting. Make it very bright if you want to see something while you are outdoors or in a well-lit room. On the other hand, if you're in a dimly lit room, reducing brightness is better.

5. Adjust the White/Black Density settings if you see them.

   ▪ White Density. Some advanced tablets, including the Samsung Galaxy Tab, allow you to set the level of white; choose an intensity that makes it easy to see items on the screen, but not so overwhelming that the white "blooms" over onto other elements, making them less attractive or harder to read. See Figure 13-2.

   ▪ Black Density. This is mostly a matter of preference. I prefer a solid and dense black. You're adjusting the intensity of the illumination behind the screen. Make it very bright if you want to see something while you are outdoors or in a very well-lit room. On the other hand, browsing the web or reading a book at night in a dimly lit room is more comfortable with lowered brightness.

6. Adjust the Color Saturation setting. There is no right or wrong choice, but try saturation slightly higher than the mid-point on the slider. Too far down and colors seem washed out, too far up and colors look garish and unnatural. But that's just me. Choice is a good thing.

7. Tap OK or Save.

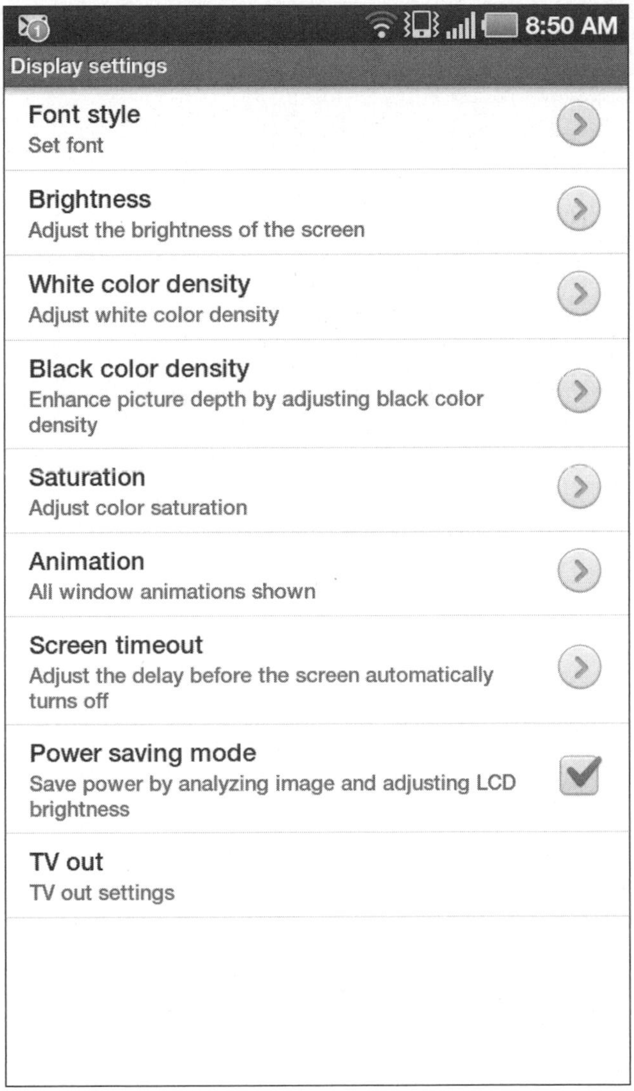

🔕 ⏱ 📶 8:50 AM

Display settings

Font style
Set font
⊙

Brightness
Adjust the brightness of the screen
⊙

White color density
Adjust white color density
⊙

Black color density
Enhance picture depth by adjusting black color density
⊙

Saturation
Adjust color saturation
⊙

Animation
All window animations shown
⊙

Screen timeout
Adjust the delay before the screen automatically turns off
⊙

Power saving mode
Save power by analyzing image and adjusting LCD brightness
☑

TV out
TV out settings

Figure 13-1

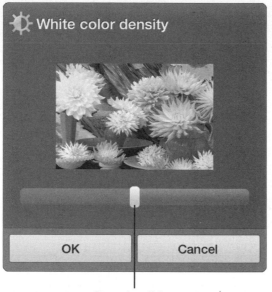

Drag the slider.

Figure 13-2

Task 2: Setting Timeouts

Nothing lasts forever. If you want to get the most time out of a battery charge, take advantage of timeout settings. Depending on your tablet, the settings will either turn off the backlight or put the entire tablet into standby after a specified time. If your tablet dims or goes into standby, you can quickly bring it back to life: Tap the screen, or quickly press the power button, or swipe across the screen. If these tricks don't work, see your tablet's instruction manual.

Here's how to adjust screen and system timeout:

1. Tap the settings icon. It may be on the tablet's home screen and called Settings, or you may have to swipe down from the frame.
2. Tap Display Settings (or Screen, or another similar tool name).
3. Tap 90 or 120 seconds for the Backlight Time-Out setting. See Figure 13-3. Experiment to find which setting works best. If the time is too short, your screen will constantly dim, even if you are sitting there reading a page; if you go too long, battery power will be a-wasting.
4. Tap 2 Minutes for the Standby Time-Out setting. Again, you don't want to go too short or too long. If this is too short a time, come back and choose a longer option. See Figure 13-4.
5. Tap OK or Save.

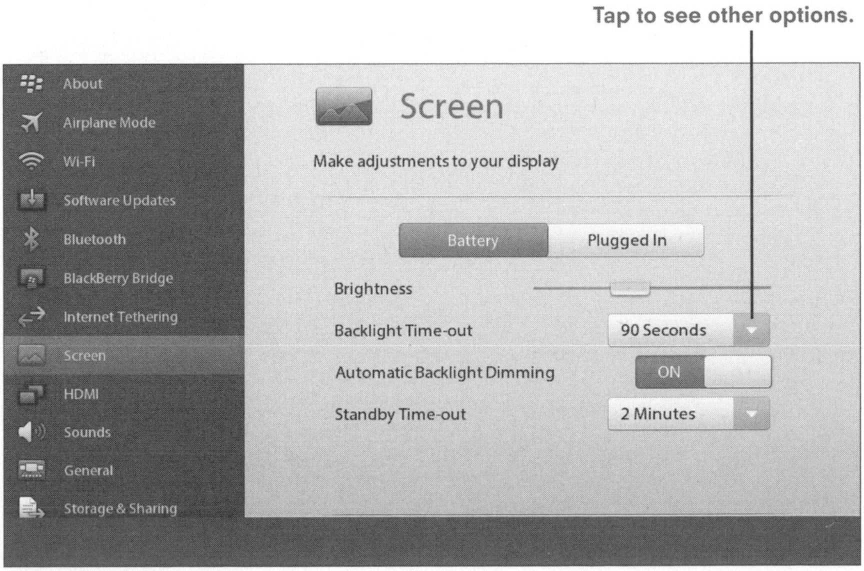

Tap to see other options.

Figure 13-3

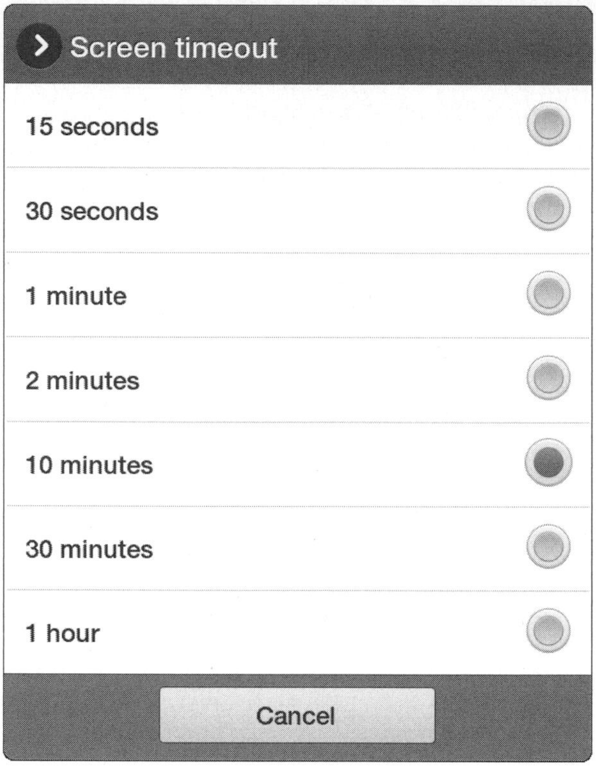

Figure 13-4

Task 3: Fixing the Clock

On most tablets, all you have to do to ensure proper time keeping is set your time zone. And on some tablets you don't even need to do that: Those devices can figure out where they are based on a WiFi router or cellphone tower signal. But, sometimes we move from place to place. I move around a lot.

Here's how to set the clock in your tablet, adjust it if you travel, or have it check for the time:

1. Tap the settings icon. It may be on the tablet's home screen and called Settings, or you may have to swipe down from the frame.

2. Tap Date & Time (or Date and Time, or Clock, or another similar name).

3. Tap the Time Zone setting (or tap the arrow next to it). Choose the setting for where you are. You'll usually see a name for the zone and a number that indicates the offset from Greenwich Mean Time; Eastern Time, for example, is -5 hours earlier than the time in London. See Figure 13-5.

4. Tap the Use 24-Hour Time setting. Choose to turn it to On or Off. Most people in America and Canada describe time in 12-hour chunks with an a.m. or p.m.: 2:32 p.m. is nap time after lunch, for example. In many other places, that same moment is expressed in 24-hour indication, as 14:32. You can choose either system.

5. Tap the Set Date and Time Automatically setting. Choose to turn it to On or Off. If you choose On, your tablet will get calendar and clock information from the Internet or a cellphone tower. If you choose Off, most tablets will let you set the date and time. See Figure 13-6.

6. Tap Date Format. Some tablets, including many Android-based devices, let you choose the style. For example, December 31, 2012, could be expressed as 12/31/2012, or as 31/12/2012, or as 2012/12/31.

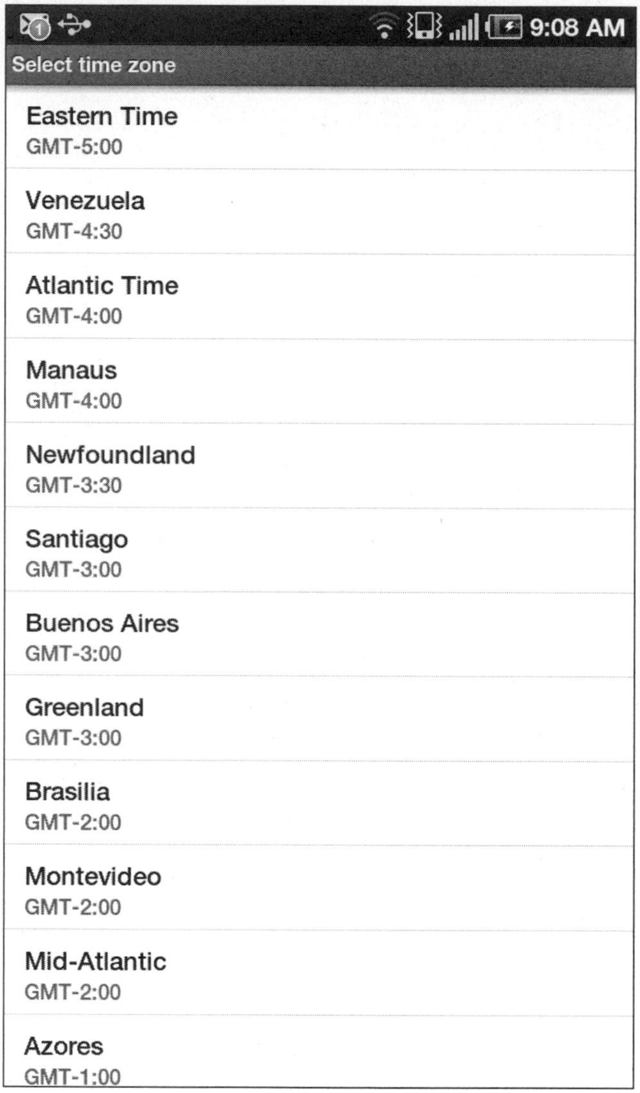
9:08 AM
Select time zone
Eastern Time
GMT-5:00
Venezuela
GMT-4:30
Atlantic Time
GMT-4:00
Manaus
GMT-4:00
Newfoundland
GMT-3:30
Santiago
GMT-3:00
Buenos Aires
GMT-3:00
Greenland
GMT-3:00
Brasilia
GMT-2:00
Montevideo
GMT-2:00
Mid-Atlantic
GMT-2:00
Azores
GMT-1:00
Figure 13-5

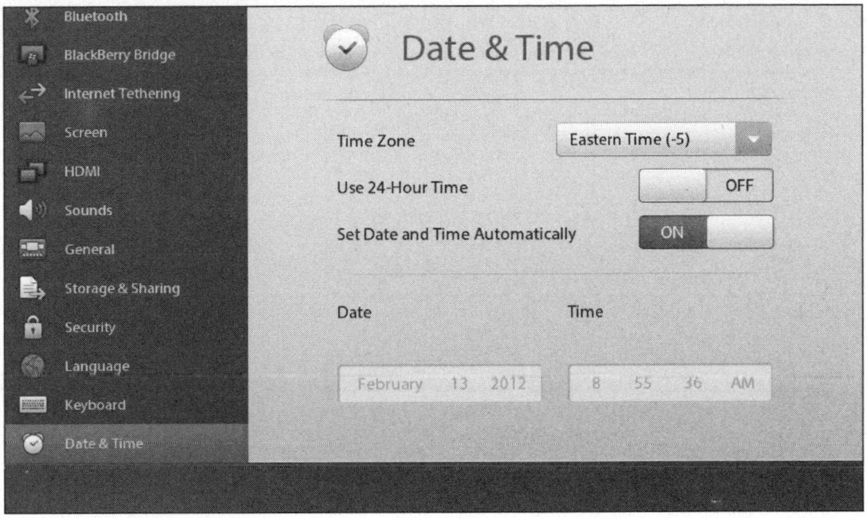
Bluetooth
BlackBerry Bridge
Internet Tethering
Screen
HDMI
Sounds
General
Storage & Sharing
Security
Language
Keyboard
Date & Time
Date & Time
Time Zone
Eastern Time (-5)
Use 24-Hour Time
OFF
Set Date and Time Automatically
ON
Date
Time
February 13 2012
8 55 36 AM

Figure 13-6

Task 4: Setting the Alarm

You can use your highly sophisticated tablet as a portable alarm clock. The great thing is that you can customize it to coordinate with your calendar, you can make it show a custom message, or you can have it play different music or noises for different events.

And it's all done with a few taps of a finger. Not all options are available on all tablets. Here's how:

1. Depending on your tablet, do one of these things:
   - Tap the clock face on the home screen.
   - Tap the digital time at the top of the home screen.
   - Tap the Alarm Clock or similarly named app on the home screen.
   - Tap the calendar app on the home screen.

2. Create an alarm event. For example, you can type a subject for reminder, decide whether to make it a one-time or recurring event, assign a location, and add a comment.

3. Tap Ring Tone or Alarm Sound. Typical selections include jaunty "good morning" jingles, lyrical and romantic tunes, and (my favorite) threatening growls. Some tablets can vibrate instead of make sounds. Don't laugh: A jiggling tablet is a good way to set alarms without disturbing other people. It should be the law for movie theaters and concert halls. See Figure 13-7.

4. Choose the clock face style. See Figure 13-8.

Depending on your tablet and the settings you chose, when the alarm goes off, your tablet's screen may have a reminder message. Tap Dismiss (or Cancel or a similar command) to stop the alarm.

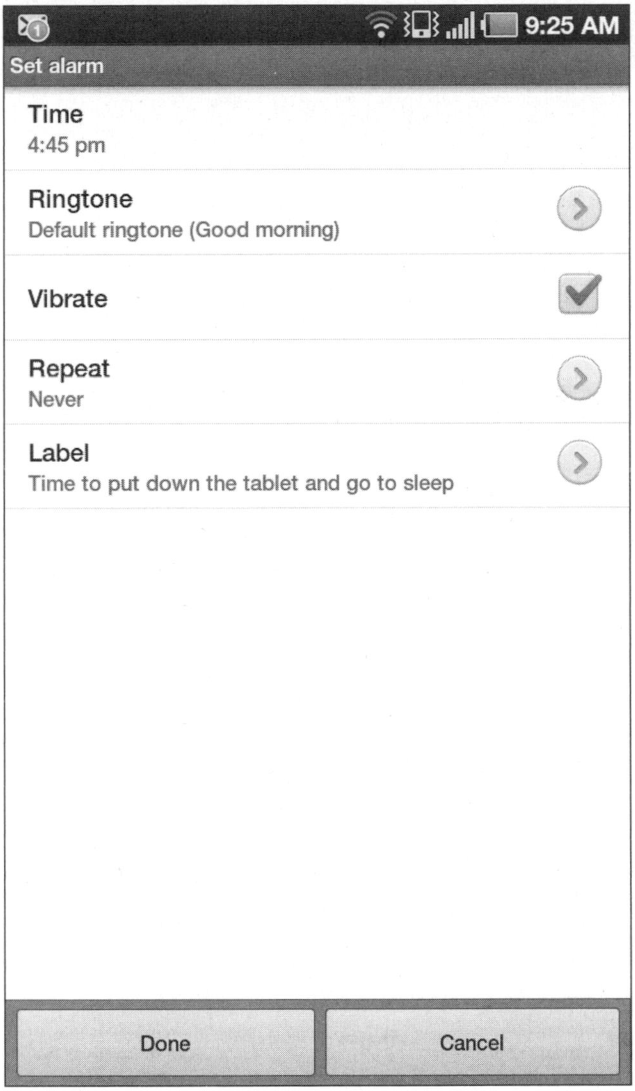
9:25 AM
Set alarm
Time
4:45 pm
Ringtone
Default ringtone (Good morning)
Vibrate
Repeat
Never
Label
Time to put down the tablet and go to sleep
Done
Cancel

Figure 13-7

Swipe left or right to see other options.

Figure 13-8

Task 5: Doing the Math

A tablet is so entertaining that you may forget that it is a computer. Because it is a computer, it loves to work with numbers. Nearly every tablet comes with a calculator (or more) — much more capable than the ones we first met at the dawn of the electronic age. Sure, you can add up your grocery bill. But most calculators can also convert between just about any type of weight, length, area, temperature, power, and speed — and some things you never have even thought to measure. The BlackBerry PlayBook's is one of the more attractive and useful calculators; other tablets have similar versions.

Here's how to use a tablet calculator:

1. Tap the calculator app icon on the home screen.
2. Tap the calculator you want to use. The BlackBerry PlayBook will show you different designs when you swipe down from the top frame and include these options:
   - Standard (addition, subtraction, multiplication, division, and some other basic operations)
   - Scientific (with advanced operators including trigonometric and numerical powers)
   - Tip (enter bill total, gratuity percentage, and the number of people who will divide the bottom line)
3. Tap the keypad to enter the numbers. See Figure 13-9.

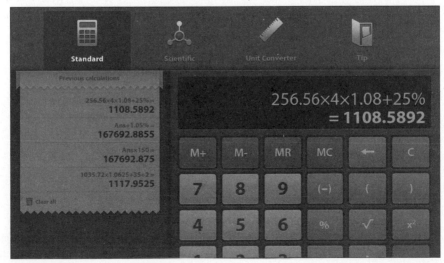

Figure 13-9

Task 6: Converting Numbers

Just the other day, some kid had the nerve to stop me on the street and ask me, "Sir, could you please tell me how many tablespoons there are in 486 cubic centimeters?" I could have spent an hour or so giving him a lesson in metric capacity and U.S. apothecary measurements. Instead, I whipped out my BlackBerry PlayBook and went to the conversion page. I chose the volume gizmo, and had the answer in two swipes and three taps: 32.4 tablespoons.

The BlackBerry PlayBook has a unit converter. For other tablets, you can get a converter at the app store. Here's how to use a conversion tool:

1. Tap the calculator app icon on the home screen.
2. Tap the menu and then tap the conversion module.
3. Touch and swipe to select a measurement.
4. Tap the form of the original number.
5. Tap the form for the unit to which you want to convert. For example, to convert from Celsius to Fahrenheit, swipe or tap Celsius for Input and Fahrenheit for Output. See Figure 13-10.
6. Type the known number. The converted answer will appear.

Figure 13-10

Task 7: Going to Flight Mode

"Ladies and gentlemen, the captain has turned on the fasten seatbelt sign. Please make sure your seat back and folding tray are in their full, upright position. At this time, we request that all mobile phones, pagers, radios and remote-controlled toys be turned off for the full duration of the flight, as these items might interfere with the navigational and communication equipment on this aircraft."

Ah, but as soon as you are in the air, the cabin is filled with people reading books on Kindles, Kobos, NOOKs, and other devices with funny names. Airlines are trying to avoid the very, very remote possibility that an electronic device with an antenna will interfere with the plane's equipment. The solution: Use your tablet in flight mode. It turns off all radios but you can still read eBooks, play built-in games, and perform other tasks that do not require communication with the outside world.

Here's how to turn on flight mode:

1. Tap the flight mode app icon (or airplane mode, or something similarly named) on the home screen.
2. Tap On for the Flight Mode setting.
3. When you are back on the ground, go back to the same app and choose Off for the Use Flight Mode setting. See Figure 13-11.

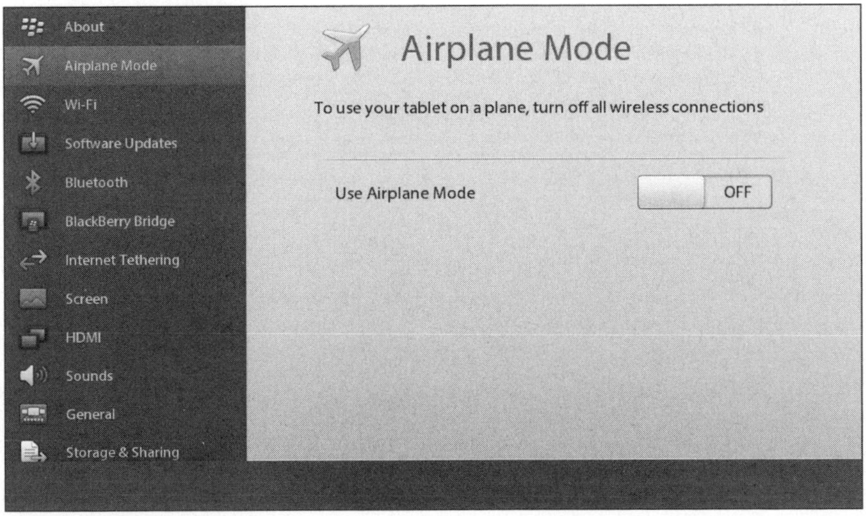

Figure 13-11

If your tablet does not have this app on the home screen, follow these steps:

1. Tap the settings icon from the home screen.
2. Tap the WiFi or Communications menu.
3. Tap Off for the WiFi setting.
4. Tap Off for the Bluetooth and Cellular settings, if your tablet offers them. See Figure 13-12.
5. When you are back on the ground, go back to the same menus and tap On.

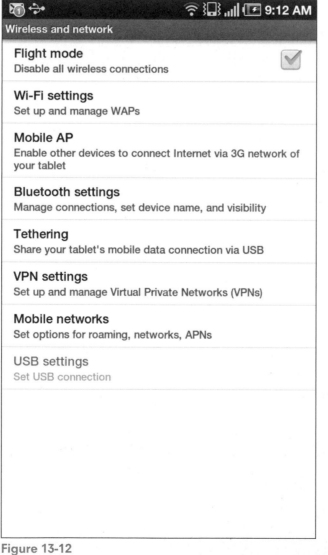

Figure 13-12

Flying with WiFi

Why do flight attendants insist that you turn off all radio systems when more and more airlines are selling WiFi connections on board their planes? Excellent question. WiFi signals are relatively weak and not likely to cause any problem with equipment on the plane. Airlines are also quite happy when they can find any way to earn a bit more from their passengers.

Cellular communication is more of an issue. If you think about it, if you turned on your cellphone (or use your tablet's cellular data link to go to the Internet) while flying at 30,000 feet, your device just might try to communicate with dozens of cell towers down below. That might cause a problem. If you use onboard WiFi and your tablet has a cellular data radio, you should turn WiFi *on* and Cell *off*.

Index